Let There Be Light in Darkness

Let There Be Light in Darkness

BY Asif Shakoor

ILLUSTRATED BY
Sharon H. Hornstein
AND Asif Shakoor

RESOURCE *Publications* · Eugene, Oregon

LET THERE BE LIGHT IN DARKNESS

Resource Publications
An Imprint of Wipf and Stock Publishers
199 W. 8th Ave., Suite 3
Eugene, OR 97401

www.wipfandstock.com

PAPERBACK ISBN: 978-1-5326-9907-8
HARDCOVER ISBN: 978-1-5326-9908-5
EBOOK ISBN: 978-1-5326-9909-2

Manufactured in the U.S.A.   10/31/19

Contents

Introduction

We all become poets when we filter reality into meaningful existence and create the world through our awareness. Spiritual poetry opens the doors to the will and lets the purity of light walk into the soul. It is osmotic with our emotional nature, bringing harmony between our inner and outer world. Poetry is an expression of nature's beauty transforming the world through our creative imagination.

A true poet sees the world with simplicity of design and brings to surface passions imbued with wisdom. I do not consider myself a poet, but an observer who takes each moment of knowledge and moves the conscious eye to probe deeper into reality. Much of the work I put on these papers is meditative, bound in the spirituality of a Sufi mystic. As a young boy growing up in Pakistan the words and style of my writing took form. The vivid beauty of nature's creation lay in the foothills of majestic mountains and made their indelible imprint on my soul.

Spiritual poetry pours into perception like words that flow through the open rivers of the heart. A poet sees through the veil of certainty, seeking the truth that gives substance to his being. In silence one learns

to hear the sounds of the world to give his
words the voice of wisdom.

Often writing becomes difficult when one
transcends the boundaries of the mind's eye,
losing sight of the creative Self. Insight into
mystic thought becomes mindful when one
unites with the fragment of the greater whole.
Most poetry of any kind looks through the mirrors
of self-reflection, giving form to the reflective
light of reason. In our tangled web of intellectual
curiosity, we must live today and seek
simplicity in our journey through life.

"Let There Be Light In Darkness" has been my
search to nurture the mind to seek deep fulfillment
in healthy living. I have used light as my metaphor
for eye-opening self-examination, striving for
greater understanding in meaning and purpose
of life. The use of the word "Darkness"
is my means of overcoming human fallacies,
suffering and give hope to humanity by striving
for great love and peace. Through writing
one can learn to overcome pain, accept
the wisdom in sorrow, overcome hatred,
and learn to forgive the unforgivable.
Through writing one can learn to overcome
greed by living through the poverty of
others, to overcome the pitfalls of success
by striving to live simply. Also, one
should seek to touch the soul of God by

acting through the righteousness
of deeds.

In writing poetry, one hopes to see
the world in all its forms. The pitfall
of writing is that one becomes his
worst critic. I have edited these
poems a dozen times and every
time I have changed them they
have escaped deeper into my
consciousness. At last I am at the
mercy of my readers and they shall
be the judge of what I have written.
The pen has written the will of the
mind. I no longer hold the wisdom
of this poet who has written on empty
pages the spirit of his awakening. I
hold no secrets; these words have
been my light in darkness and yours
for the taking.

The work would never have come into
fruition without the gracious effort and
inspiration by several important people
working on this project. I would like first
to thank my family for their sacrifices and
support in this very time-consuming process.
I would also like to thank Thelma J.
White and Babar Shakoor for their monumental
effort in editing and providing constructive criticism.
They helped me pull the work together and pushed

me to polish and smooth out the rough edges.
I am also very grateful to Sharon H. Hornstein
for her enthusiasm, heart, and soul that she put
in my words with her great artistic talents
and wonderful illustration. I owe them
my deepest gratitude, for they kept me
from giving up the task and motivated
me to pursue and complete
this work.

Consciousness

The hands of the wind uproot the
fragrance that these flowers have
no will to keep. In the deep hue of
color, life dissolves into the illusions of
the senses. In true love a rose is born
and the heart is all-giving. When will
you become conscious of your rose?
In your hand the world is hope.
When will you become conscious
of your real world in hope? Human
nature is restless and moves against
time. When will you become
conscious of your space in time?

A life that is tangled in doubt fails to
move beyond stagnation. When
will you become conscious of your
doubtful living? True beauty lives
under the vision of a mystical poet.
When will you become conscious of that
which is beautiful? The journey through
life is a path of many directions.
When will you become conscious of
your destined path?
Will your soul awaken and let the
conscious eye see into your righteousness?
When will you become conscious
of your consciousness?

Let There Be Light

Oh, light, you have traveled
far to tell these eyes your
forgotten story. In the
strong will to move, you burn
away the darkness from this
world to reveal your eternal
truth. In humble ways, you
permeate the soul to illuminate
the heart. Will you come,
wash away the sorrows that
burden the spirit, and
live free?

Oh, light! Will you become the
seeds of eternity to awaken love
for the great soul? In silence of
the night, you are many shades
of poetic mystery. The beauty of
nature sleeps in your arms, and
all of life bow to your artistic
vision. Your spirit is restless and
your will strong, for revelation
is constant, unforgiving; Your
burning passion warms the
world and gives birth to the
face of humanity.

Your light enters the mind's
eye and opens the door to
consciousness. Dear light, you

have finally come home to
rest, and the world is all
luminous colors. In moments of
total blindness, even darkness
will shed your light. Let there be
light to see yourself fully reflected
on the surface of hard reality.
Will you grow out of this
light and run away from
your creation? Oh, light, can
you give me the moment to look
in and out of you? Your world
is all that I see, and your light of
reason in this spirit grows. Let
there be light in darkness
as wisdom spreads to the
world it knows.

Half-Forgotten

In the warm haze of noon,
the clock holds you fast
in time. The sun embraces
you in full blaze of glory,
and the lemonade half-
empties your thirst.
Children skip beats on
concrete squares as
the rhythm of laughter
comes into full play.
In hot, humid air this
music drums through the
dense concrete landscape.
In the fullness of reality, the
wind stirs emotions, calms
the senses. From the open
windows of passing cars,
cigarette smoke rises in a
corkscrew dance.

Open hydrants flood the
streets; water gushes out in full
blast. Children bathe in the
soothing joy of cold, silky
water drowned in laughter.
The old sit on benches;
dogs wag their tails. Pairs of
runners dash through the
park like fugitives seeking
the next world. The summer
breeze catches you by surprise,
holds your face to the sun that warms
your spirit. You sit on the soft,
humble grass eating fruit

that is sweet and raw.
Memories melt into the
day like ice cream that waits
too long to be eaten. The day
is half gone, the world,
half forgotten.

Butterflies lift their wings into
the sacred blue sky. The soul
breathes in the splendor of nature,
nurtured in the honey of sweet
emotions. In far, open fields trees
pose in graceful forms, opening
their beauty to the warmth of the
majestic sun. Half past noon, the
spirit is freed as time runs away
from your winding road. You
can almost see the past moving
slowly across your mind, as
you reflect in this silent moment.

Beneath this cool shaded tree
flickers the shadow of your sculptured
face. The benches are now empty,
but children still come out to play on
this aged street, their laughter echoing
through your memory-painted reality.
The clock's hands have stopped,
but your will for time moves on,
noon closing into night as memories
settle like dust under the mist
of twilight. Will you cleanse
the darkness from your eyes
and immerse your spirit
in light?

The Soul of Night

In the mist that blankets the
forest rest mountains that
sleep in their frozen state.
Twilight falls like a heavy hand,
awakening the soul of night.
Hold the silence within;
listen to the wind that
taunts and flirts with slow
moving rivers. In serenity of
dreams the conscious eye
sees into the heart of nature.
Will the stars burn away eternal
time as their will surrenders
to the abyss of darkness?

Trees stand with pride, and
flicker, flutter, flaunt their
leaves as the soft hand of the
wind moves them to laughter.
The night has called your
name and the deep mystical
voice stirs your calm spirit.
Will you come into the forest
and touch the mighty fallen
tree? The moon sparkles in
a half-broken ring, unwitting
bride to the desires of the
night. In shady mood of silver-
gray, true love blankets
the cold mysterious world.

Under the soft ivory
glow, nature veils its virgin
beauty that comes to full bloom
before dawn awakens to
the morning light.

Open the doors to your heart
and let nature become
the only guest. Let the mist
fall like thirst-filled
dew-drops that dip
into the lips of red roses.
Night comes to an
end; the forest comes
to life with full colors.
The world washes away the
darkness under the light of the
golden sun. The morning
breaks through the open sky
and hangs over jagged mountains
as slow-moving clouds burden the
wind, cutting into snowy peaks.
The inner eye of nature becomes
the prism through which light
paints infinite colors into the open
landscape. The forest is lost to
the trees; the trees have
become the forest. In mirrors
that reflect the soul of
night lies one's true nature.

Will you come out of
your old ways and let
Nature become your
spiritual teacher?

Heaven

I exist for your imagination.
Will you let me walk deeply into
the crevices of your mind
where eternal love is layered
in abundance? You are the
blood of my living form
and a flickering candlelight
in a world full of dreams.
Why won't you let me read
the tender emotions that are
written in your heart? Time
has sculpted your face with
beauty that holds me prisoner
for all eternity. In my unspoken words,
I will call out your name to the wind.
These words are rivers that flood
the ocean with emotions.
There is no surface that can
hold you beneath it. In your
blood my spirit is born to run free
from the world. I long to walk in your
soul to reach your heart. Will you
remember me in your moments
when my eyes felt your eternity come
to light? The hand's touch burns in
the glow of consciousness. The darkness
of this world blankets your
form as your spirit grows
in the candle's eye.

Hands fold in prayer and the cup
fills your faith with the wholeness
of life. Forget not that the thirst
for existence is deeper than the
ocean. Stars' glitter is reflected
in the white matter of your eyes, as
moonlight paves the road to Heaven.
In the calm tranquility of your
fragrance, the gentle breeze holds you
in its hands. I will take you in with every
breath and never breathe against the
yearning to love. The light of my existence
absorbed in your charcoal eyes
reflects the full surrender of my
soul. Will you come into
these doors that break through
your hard shell of reality? In silence
we make our journey under the
will of unbroken love. If I can
escape the will of this world,
your love will take me
into Heaven above.

Mongolian Moon

The moon has come out of
hiding, and the clouds bow in full
awareness. Like a white-spotted
tiger, it roars through the fullness
of its Mongolian face. Lovers hide
in the moonlight and embrace
each other through the night. All
is revealed in the landscape of
gray-black shades of mystery.
The moon sprinkles white silver
dust and pulls the river's black
silky water. Into the deep calm,
the wind stirs the spirits of
nature as the moon reflects its
seductive charm.

Mountains soar into the sky,
longing to pierce the heart of
the moon; like a bloodthirsty arrow
that breaks from the bow seeking
the one it loves. The path through
darkness the moonlight chisels
away, softly carving the night into
beauty and form. This silent world
is full of sounds, as the warm hand
of the summer breeze awakens the
world from deep dreams. The sun
sheds light on the moon's dusky face
as the clouds try to hide all its blemishes.
In the early morning light, the moon
is drowned and eclipsed in the deepness
of blue sky. Let the moon roll on
the finger of creation and become the
axis of life's true purpose.

Oh, open-minded spirit! Will you
let the moon awaken the human
consciousness and hold it in
your mystical spell? Were you not
born through the rib of Mother Earth?
You are the child of this Earth, as
you circle in hope, longing for your
one true love. The full moon gives face
to the mystical sky, a white pearl
to the naked eye. Will you look
through the darkness of this
world to seek the moon that
touches the sky?

Into Beauty

We sit in a café and look each
other over. Your eyes are gentle,
and the tea is in a mist of smoke.
We talk of beauty, your well-
versed song. Your face is soft;
your black silky hair is free-
flowing and your body warm.
This is all they see under the skin
of their eyes. In their will for total
surrender, they will love with full
emotions, but you blind them with
your beauty. Why so lonely now?
Give them what they want until
there is no more to give. This
savage lust is the slave of many;
you weaken them to
their knees.

Your voice breaks, and the heart is
unsettled; there are none who now
look your way. Your pulse runs to
your face with a sensual glow. Your
eyes look for comfort in wandering
eyes. The light has unveiled the mask
of truth: You have become too
opaque to the soul of this world.
Are you afraid that the real you
can never be real? What will you do
when old age robs you of your tender
form? In mirrors of self-reflection,
the surface no longer holds your true
reality. You have become like the
still wind, neither
seen nor felt.

Delusions! The whole world
is a delusion. When will the real
face of beauty break face with thee?
A black cover catches my eye,
hardbound and rectangular with
vivid colors, but that is not T. S. Eliot.
We talk in soft and soothing words
as your fragrance breathes life
into the café. In your self-conscious
stares, you sense the self-possessed
will that you know so well. You
hold me prisoner with your eyes.
Your unconscious form sets the
beat and many fall into your
trap, but I escape with my final
verse intact. Run away! Run away!
The voice of reason calls to me as
my heart is thumping and
keeps looking back.

By SHAKOUR

Breathless

Light burns your darkness, and
you become the ashes of your
form. Breathe, just breathe, and there
will be so much yet to breathe. If you
reflect into the moment, you will
be swallowed whole in time that
holds you deep. In your gluttonous
ways, your fate will be written by your
forgotten ways. What becomes of a
flower that never awakens to the
world of all possibilities? What
becomes of emotions that drown
you in the depths of your ocean?
Skin deep is the flesh of reality
that bleeds into rivers where
dreams flow into the conscious
eye. Just breathe, take it all in,
and let it transform your
will to breathe.

The mystical voice stirs the wind
and calls nature to breathe life
into the barren landscape. Into
the valley blows the cold north
wind and the spirit shivers and
quivers to stay warm in the hard
cold surface of existence. Under
the web of your consciousness, there
is no escape, and the trap is set for the
life you will come to live. Breathe

in deeply, hold it against your
will, and your breath will lift
your spirit into the sky. Will you
breathe into your soul and let it
become your conscious
storm?

In the caves of your being, the echo will
whisper your name, and time will hold
your world strong. Just remember
that trees will breathe into their
light of creation and hold you in their
joy. Like a fire that grows through
love, you will breathe your lover
whole. How long will you chase
the wind that holds no beginning,
no end? Let your emotions fan
your flames and awaken the light of
your inner being. Have you forgotten
that the forest must burn once
more to give life a second chance?
The air is thick, and you breathe it
with hungry passion. Why do you hold
your silence and breathe it in no more?
The beauty of the world will leave
you breathless; open your senses
and close the door.

Wanderer

The silent moment
implodes onto itself to
take you in. Memories
burst out into a thousand
sparks like shattered dreams
against the hard glass of reality.
The night falls into the open
hands of time and ferments with
decay of age. We were once young,
but now there are only traces
of forgotten moments that echo
against the walls of consciousness.
Someone is walking from afar toward
your destined path. Will you trace
your fading steps to search for the
end in your beginning? What
can a heart seek in this
truth of love but the soul
of the living?

Bridge to Love

Will you build me a bridge that
reaches your door?
A slow-moving river flows into me,
but my heart is full of storms.
We are but an ocean apart. Will you walk across
this bridge? I will never be far.
In this dark night, the wind is cold! How will I find
you among these distant stars?
Your hand has touched my hand, and the
bridge is complete.
We stand tall in a frozen dance as water
rests under our feet.

Child in Man

Life comes into full bloom, and
the child grows into the man.
In the footsteps of time, you
travel like a ghost that comes
and goes with every flickering
moment. In your conscious
awakening, you come to
realize that there is no
turning back the
will of time.

Your heart is heavy, and there is
conformity in your will to be
free. You face rustic light, but
your eyes still reflect your
youthful ways. In the stream
of consciousness, the shadow
will walk toward the footprints
of manhood. The son will
awaken the child inside the
man, with strong spirit to
be understood.

Shameless

Call him out as he hides his
shame deep in his heart. Will
you lift your burden against
the wind and surrender your
soul to the wings of freedom?
You play the fool, eating the
unripe fruit before its time.
Why fear the light that cuts
deep into your naked face?
In your eyes you lose the
vision that seeks the forbidden
truth. Will you ever find your
road when you walk blindly
and hold no ground? The path to
simple wisdom crumbles at your
feet and burns the house full of
pride. A bowl full of water
unsettles and trembles in
your hands.

You spill more with your thirst than
what you hope to drink. Will you break
the heart that holds your spirit
against walls of freedom? The joy to
live free holds no shame. Guilt
oppressed by human nature, freedom
never comes to blame. Can you
walk through the needle's eye with no
hindrance to the world and thread
through your two ends of existence?

How will you tie the loose ends
of your broken fate with no
knots attached to your reality?
Will you forgive the soul that
denies the body
its truth?

When will you crack the shell of
consciousness and come out fully
formed? Night blankets and warms
your spirit, but your true Self is
seen in the dust of dawn. Will you
walk toward the shaded tree and sit to
reflect in this moment of eternity? Your
face is wrinkled with time, but your eyes
still reflect the shame of human wisdom.
How will you come to see this world
of humanity that no longer
holds your vision?

Neighborhood

I have known these eyes that
found light in moments of time
past. They are the white marrow
of my childhood, deeply rooted in
the footsteps of my beginning. The
story of forgotten youth, written
in the cracks of concrete weathered
with age, tells of simpler times.

The dirty, yellow-bricked homes with
bellowing, smoked-filled chimneys
resting on narrow streets still
welcome the child lost in youth. Hot
humid summers with sensuous breezes
still burn through my senses. The
stars of the night still come out under the
wide-open sky that gave wonder to childhood
dreams. I can still recall the half-forgotten
faces that looked down from high-rise
windows through the iron bars of
inner-city concrete jungle.

Now the rust of reality framed in every
window stares at the world with silent,
mocking gazes. These houses stand side by
side with rigid faces, cold eyes, and closed
doors, swallowing humanity in the coldness
of winter. The sun moved shadow to
play on sidewalks carved in squares.
In endless time, children skipped over

lines and played ball free-willed with
no thought for tomorrow. Was
it heads or tails, you recalled, when the
quarter was flicked into the air by your
nervous thumb? How often did you
win the bet? Raindrops fell like pearls
from heaven as you lifted your head, arms
bare and twisted, totally absorbed in your
whirlwind dance. Full of backstreet
revelations, the school walls dazzled
with spray-painted graffiti that you
could read like a book.

I know these eyes that blur the boundaries
of past and present. They are the reflection
of human spirit that lived and died a thousand
times. Weathered emotions washed
into rivers of nightly dreams are reborn
into reality. The senses still taste
the aroma of golden honey-crusted bread
when I passed by the corner bakery.
The fruit market with fresh green apples,
and ripe yellow bananas still lingers
in the aftertaste of childhood pleasures.
The red bricks stand against time,
but the mortar now crumbles in a
hand that is mature and strong. The
passing days of many years have
rolled back the neighborhood with
childhood memories. I know the joy that
echoes through my past and calls the inner

boy to come out and play. The wind has
broken my silent steps, concrete
sidewalks have softened into clay,
steps no longer silent as heavy
emotions begin to stray.

Forbidden

In your forbidden state, you are
not to have what you have been
forbidden. You look at life with a
forbidden face. In your forbidden
passion, you call love great. Those
who have tasted the forbidden
fruit will no longer fear the bitter
poison of reason. The senses hold
no morality when the senses sense their
sensual state. There is no substance
in reality when eyes are blinded
by the light of wisdom. Why anchor
oneself to dreams in an ocean that
has no surface? Fear forbids one
to mock his shame and hold human
grace above pride. The wind
forbids him from breathing the air
that is morbid, full of sorrow.

Will you break your silence and let the
forbidden thought escape through
the conscious mind? The echo of
reality is reflecting back from the
walls of your cave. In the water that
reveals the soul, your eyes will mirror
your forbidden face. God forbids
the killing of soul when the body's
rituals become godless. Why
search for hidden treasures that
are nowhere to be found? In

the glass prism of reality, the shadow burns, and the ashes of form become the forbidden truth. Only a fool will touch the fire that burns with the spirit of true love. What you will never have can never be owned. You are forbidden to take that which can never be taken. A rising wave that heaves with emotions, your mind spills into the forbidden abyss. You are caught in your own web, like a fish trapped in unseen water. Will you seek your forbidden fate that destiny will come to slaughter?

Time in Hand

Let time come to your door and
become the guest for all eternity.
With time you'll walk far and
wide on the surface of your
conscious journey. In every grain
of time, one's hands will hold
it close before it slips and falls.
Let it cleanse the soot of this world
that settles into the depth of the
senses. In the past, time came to bury
you whole, but in the present, you'll
live these moments toward tomorrow.
The spirit of night is born in your
eyes, and only time can hold you
in your dreams. Oh, time! Why have
you become empty-handed
and give no more?

Memories lay wasted in your conscious
backdrop, and there is no time to reflect
on passing moments. The dust of time
settles on the soul, and the spirit within
buffs them clean. How much time
will you borrow to pay your debt?
You have looked far into these empty,
twisted roads for the one you seek.
They have folded and given way
with every step. In the light of your
eyes, every voyage is a comfort to
the soul. Will you break your

calm for the guest that time brings
to your door? Will you have time
to seek the passion of your being?

You have become the mist in the
morning light. Will you let destiny
rub the space between your shadow
and form? Let the seething smoke
rise from your spirit and give the wind
a moment of self-realization. Will the
window to your spirit fail to open
when you hope to part with time?
In days of autumn, shed your
true nature and bear your form. In
winter, shake and shiver in your
winter coat. In spring, plant
the seeds of nature to bring
the colors and life once
more to the world.
In your every step walks the
summer breeze, the hot sun melts
into your human vulnerability.
Listen to the wind echoing time's
fading laughter. Time keeps all
moments and you are given but one
moment to keep. Oh, time, in your
beginning are the seeds of humanity,
but toward your end there will only be
the light of human truth. Will you
spare this withered soul and give
it the wisdom to grow
old in youth?

Father to Son

You breathe me into this world
with all your glory. A touch
of your soul rests in my
heart. In your hands, you mold
my existence, but it is your love
that gives me form. Reflected
in the mirror of your eyes is
the light of my spirit. Your
chiseled face is etched in
frozen time, ageless, eternal.
There is so much feeling buried in
those layers of moments as the boy
looked into the man, and the
man into the boy.

How much water can one
hold in one's ocean? Oh,
Father! Will you let me walk
into your world and find comfort
in your firm footsteps? The
breath of life gives me joy,
every breath a gift from
God. There is so much room
and comfort under the shadow
of your being. There is so much
light that glows through your eyes
and guides the spirit though its
darkest path. Those were fleeting
moments when we danced under

the falling raindrops and
held the world close to our existence.

Will you sleep under the comfort
of your beginning? Days get lost
into nights like withered leaves that
are stripped, torn, and broken by the
autumn breeze. Oh, proud age, you
linger too long in our somber faces.
Know you not that the bird
has outlived its caged existence?
The wings long to touch the sky, and
the blazing sun is full of earthly
glory. The child has walked into the
shadow of man. In light that holds
time still, how you live, wisdom
will come to plan.

Heartfelt Being

There you stood in your frozen state where
time distills day into night.
These unforgiving hands have chiseled your
form into solid emotions, bringing my soul to light.
Gray sandstones of time, aged lines
are etched on your graceful old face
by rivers that part these mountains
flowing deep-hearted, fast, and cold.
The child sheds the fragrance of laughter, but in
man, only silence he hears.
True happiness holds no treasure. Let it remain
buried for a thousand years.
In one moment, you are born in conscious form,
molded by these hands in clay.
Oh, fleeting youth, you have left too soon when
so much life is still in play.
Oh, aged wisdom, the spirit is calling to ask what meaning
you hold in this ill-fated life.
Can happiness ever come into being when the body
and soul live in strife?
Awaken! Let the rhythm of your steps find
natural harmony the teacher.
I am neither man nor woman, but one
imperfect humble creature.

Prisoner of Will

Your spirit has become restless.
You are caged in the iron will of
freedom. Trapped in space, you
have become empty of form. In
constant motion, you remain
wild, untested and without rhythm
in your steps. Hardened emotions
tell your story with every muscle
that moves under the skin. The
look of sadness reflects in shallow
eyes. The soul is unbound; your
body remains savage and untamed.
Though you pace rhythmically
to and fro you still remain
unbroken in hardness of time. The
spirit of your sorrow is revealed
in your fateful life dance. The rust
of reality clings to you as thoughts grow
old and dull. With sharp moral
judgement they cut into your freedom.
The world is built on many shades of
meaning, but the world you know
is estranged. You eat what is given,
but starve for more. Hunger for
freedom will never set you free.

With their empty stares, empty
faces, and mocking eyes, the world
diminishes the substance of
of your being. Your emotions run

fast, and the light burns deep in your
conscious rituals. Your soul remains
strong, but in your shadow, darkness
has erased your name. You have
become a prisoner in body and spirit,
struggling in vain. The mind is restless
and seeks calm wisdom in storms
of thought. In freedom, one is born,
but in life he is torn and broken. Iron
bars such as these will change happiness
to grief and sorrow. Your dreams become
saturated with reality; you are awakened
into an even stranger dream. Will simple
truth erase these boundaries between
life and death? One whispers of hope as
words bring one into life, but one's
thoughts are yet impoverished. One must
let time mold thoughts from dust into
clay, forming image of consciousness.
These folded forgiving hands hold the
rituals of prayers, giving devotion to love.
Why not break through walls of oppression,
opening the doors to freedom? Then,
no longer a prisoner of will, one
becomes the wind beneath the
wings of reason.

The Darkened Hour

Today the world will be all
light. The endless glow of
bright wisdom will cast no
shadow on the soul. Time shall
come to rest in your hand, but
joy will lift it into the sky like
open-handed wings. Dissolved into
one's present is the dust of past.
The darkened hour walks in with a hot
summer breeze and thirst for life becomes
the water for tomorrow. The mind
reflects through unseeing eyes and
anticipates the footprints
of forgotten time.

Memories linger like fossilized shadows
that mold days and nights into bodily
form. The heart bleeds into the porous
mind when reason breaks away from the
emotional will. The dark night is the
hour full of dreams, as time escapes reality
through one's consciousness. The unforgiving
sun burns rivers dry and the fish will have
no home. A shadow will grow into the light
until the form has no existence. The
light will swallow darkness until
darkness has no light to devour. The
luminous soul is the mirror of
self-illusion with perception of
sense in worldly delusions. You

are nothing but a dream born
into a conception of a dream. The
shallow existence has become your
deep ocean when you drown in it a
thousand times. Silent is the tongue
that holds words under your past.

What has been spoken, your mind speaks
with freewill. The footsteps of reality are
knocking at your door but you no
longer live in your home. What unfolds
in your conscious eye is the mocking laughter
of eternity. The ashes of unfulfilled desires
burn your spirit, as emotional entropy
fuels the fire. Let the smoke rise from the
residue of sorrow so you can find grace
in your suffering. The darkened hour
is your hour to escape from time.

Will you find your true love, hidden in
your heart? Will you call to the wind to
bring back the moment that awakened
your soul? The bewildered face grows
old with age, waiting for life to give it
meaning. Like a silent guest you
walk too fast in the eternal reality of
your cosmic space. The world is in
your hand but you are two steps
behind the rhythm of your heart.
The stars burn bright but the light
of hope grows dim and the world

becomes dark in its whole. In the
deep well of time I search for
love that only reflects your
water in my soul.

Hiroshima

Scream through these wide-open eyes and hold
your face strong. In one moment, time will melt
human shame.
A bomb has been dropped on civilization
that burns red-hot orange, and nightmares come
into flames.
Cracked walls scorched and lined with human
forms, once living, now ghostly shadows in vapor
and dust.
In a heap of gold, black-carbon ash, there
lies the crater under the
mushroom crust.
Oh, withered earth you are scorched and burn
with pain.
Will you forgive human folly, as we are
no longer sane?
Landscape lies broken in two, and Mother
Nature is empty, barren and no
longer real.
Deep, silent souls walk without reason
through hollow eyes that no
longer feel.
Through the vast open sky an iron tear, heavily burdened,
single minded, fell straight into the human spirit, and your truth
awakened and cried.
You burned the peaceful world with
waves of monsoon flames, and your God has
finally died.
Scream! Let this ghostly sound chase the
cowardly wind and pierce through your
shattered heart.
What will be tomorrow when the
dust settles, and consciousness splits you into
many parts?

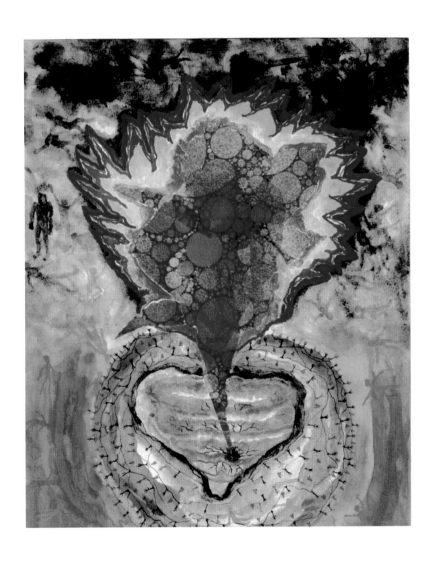

A Word Too Many

***

The thirst for water moves you closer
into your way of life.
The bowl of substance is your wisdom in
happiness and strife.

***

Look deep into yourself, and
the light will reveal the truth to
your naked eyes.
Let your spirit be awakened
through consciousness where
no reality lies.

***

Will you hold back your words before
they leave your tongue?
The wind holds fast your words until
the ears they have stung.

***

If you are afraid to take your first step, then
you will fall into doubt first and last.
Only true wisdom holds no anchor to
your present or to your past.

***

True knowledge opens the doors to your
mind and gives your senses the
wealth of experience.
True wisdom humbles to
humanity as one grows wise through
your intelligence.

***

If you live through your external world
you will destroy your internal existence.
The spirit is empty and wanders
with time.
There is no rhythm in life, no beauty,
no rhyme.
You will walk through your beginning
toward your end but cover no distance.

***

The enemy among your friends often lurks
in the dark.
Evil will come to light, but only the good
will leave their mark.

***

In your house of wisdom, your pride
will rob you blind.
How will your mind seek comfort in
emptiness left behind?

***

If you are afraid to walk beyond your steps,
then you will hold no will to bravery.
The mind is a tangled web of
reality and the soul will be sold to slavery.

***

In mystical love, the oneness of love is
toward the one who loves.
True love is divine from one below
to the one above.

***

The only treasure is the one you give
with your heart.

What you will gain is your joy in others with
every moment from the start.

***

You will walk endlessly, chasing your
greed in all directions.
How will you bargain with wealth that
fills you with affliction?

***

A thousand roads may lead to one truth, but
a wise soul acquires many truths
on roads most traveled.
On your journey, you will walk far and
wide, your truth with time will
soon unravel.

***

In wisdom, you are known like a seed
that grows into your soul.
Bring forth this cup of water and let your being
reflect in your bowl.

***

When the will of the world is
no longer free,
the truth of reality has lost its face to eyes
that no longer see.

***

If you seek knowledge, then your road
is straight and wide.
Will you shed light on ignorance and
give it no place to hide?

***

The fate of humanity comes home to rest

under the guise of being civilized.
Let there be light in your darkness; in
light hope never dies.
***

What have you become but a
mold in the hands of reality?
Will you walk toward your existence,
and touch the mighty oak tree?
***

A spirit without wisdom is like a
book without substance.
How will the truth be written
in a world that holds no justice?
***

The clever are often smart, but not
very intelligent; only humility
can bridge the gap.
Why do you weave your
own web and then fall
into your own trap?
***

Your spirit is deeply rooted in curiosity, and
grows strong in your heart of wonder.
Only an ignorant soul will chase the wind
and waste life with endless blunder.
***

The fool gives advice for a set price. A wise
man gives it freely.
Will you pay your debt to knowledge? In richness
to poverty, you will be.
***

By SHAKOOR

Find me a well of knowledge to quench
my infinite thirst.
My beginning will come tomorrow, and my
end will be my first.

***

Those who run away from the truth are
often caught in their lies.
How will you face your conscience that
rubs the truth in your eyes?

***

If your will becomes transparent, then
there is no room for deception.
What becomes of life that holds
no purpose, no direction?

***

Let your wisdom flow into your heart and
fill you with delight.
A soul that overcomes darkness is radiant
and beautiful to the sight.

***

The greatest story ever told was once
written by a book.
Will you turn the pages of time and give
your words another look?

***

A house full of books is like a heart
filled with abundance of love.
Those who seek knowledge expand
their greatness into the
universe above.

***

True, it is true that truth is your
only truth when it all
becomes true.
Wisdom, it is in your wisdom
that you grow wise when in heart
your wisdom grew.

***

A book that is never opened is like
a heart that has never felt the
pangs of love.
The journey through your imagination
awakens the spirit
to Heaven above.

***

Oh, children of this world, give me
the sorrow and hunger of
your land.
The world is blind with greed but
there in not much you can hold
in your hand.

***

If you love someone, your spirit
comes into being human.
It is this act of humanity that
binds man to woman.

***

My ashes remain long after this fire
burns to a kindle.
Oh, fair wind, put it into your hands
and send it to her.

***

A drunk that babbles the truth often
speaks from the heart.
How sober is your reality when
life plays its part?

***

There are times when moments of
realization become so near.
Throw mud in your water, shake it, and
then wait for it to clear.

***

In your drunken state, you promise never to
drink after you finish your last drink.
How deep will you escape into your thoughts
until there is no reason to think?

***

If you are afraid to fail, then you are bound
to succeed in your failure.
What will become of success when you will
not become her savior?

***

If you fall at the feet of failure
then success will never come
knocking at your door.
A life that takes pride in success
is narrow and gains
nothing more.

***

The wandering leaf drifts into
the wind and falls to the earth in
silent surrender.
Were you not born yesterday
in youth, a fleeting moment with
all your splendor?

***

We linger like faded footsteps in
dust of time, held firm in
wind's hands of serenity.
Is it not the eternal that seeks
the moment or the moment
that seeks its eternity?

***

The night walks quietly into your dreams
but in the light of dawn you are awakened
by the soft whisper of the summer breeze.
"Will you come into the light," the echo
calls to the wind, "and follow
me, please?"

***

A Mother's Burden

It was the day of the funeral. The
clock's hand softly pressed at
8:00 a.m. The heart felt
heavy, ached with sorrow, and
filled with the void of somber
emotions. The moment of
awareness had come too quickly.
In the brightly lit room, soulful
faces move with grace and sit in
their quiet space. These apparitions,
like ghostly shadows, blur the edges
of my sanity. Life's moments hold
too fast, as my spirit searches for
meaning with deep empty stares.
The maddening silence comes in like
an unwelcome guest. These eyes that
once reflected the eternal light
are forever lost to a mother's
embrace. My thoughts have become
so apprehensive that they burn through
my existence. These eyes are filled
with bitter tears and run so freely into
a world with probing eyes. The deep
wounds of reality cut deep into the
soul as the blood of humanity
spills with their lies.

Pop! Pop! Pop! The
haunting scream that shattered
the serenity of life and in one eternal

moment all came to rest on the
broken surface of reality. You
were taken away from me before I
could realize that you were truly
gone. That gun in those merciless
hands tore through a mother's
womb with ravaged fury. The
restless spirit that devours our
youth pushes them too quickly into
the grave. Will they ever see the light
of humanity in the blind rage of
civilization? How will a mother's
trembling hands wash away the blood
stains of her children? How can I let
you go my son? You are at this
moment the dearest to me. We have
shared each other's world so long.
How will I sever the bond of motherly
love that held me close to your
soul? The wings of life have lifted
you to the sky. You have become so
still and cold like a frozen rose, but
this was not your way. Who has
silenced your lips that once
spoke so elegantly? I yearn for
your awakening in a heart
that held you so reverently.

Who has the strength to calm
this mother's deep anguish? Your
childhood laughter echoes from the

stillness of your body. Will I ever be
able to fill this empty soul? I could see
the hands of the clock reach out to me
to give comfort to my broken grief.
Tick-tock, tick-tock, the rhythm of
my heartbeat marches to the steps
of your funeral procession. One
hour to go as I reflect on your
first walk; your first words still
whisper in my ears. I turn
to look at your face, and the
world becomes the voice of
cynical laughter. The Divine
light lifts you with grace, and
I give you to the Lord with
prayers, hereafter.

Your first day at school, you
came home running into these
arms with open embrace. Dear,
Lord! You have robbed me of my
total joy. Why so silent, my wholesome
dove? They lift the casket onto their
shoulders and my feet sink into the
ground. You somehow have
become so near to me, but
the burden of your stillness is
what weighs me down.

The funeral is but a moment
away, and your casket seems so

heavy now. The hands of the
clock seem so familiar now.
Lowered into the sacred ground
we come to bury the humanity of
our nation. In silence you will
sleep under this bed of great earth
as I plant the seeds of flowers at
your grave. Like a soulful gardener
these hands will nurture the
love that you once gave.

Let Me In

This soul awakened when
you walked in, stepping softly.
The door opened and
my heart was shaken
by your godly beauty. You
shed your fragrance through
your loving form and the
wind held you in its hands
like a humble servant. Dear
beloved, when will you open
your heart and let me in? The
days are cold, and my nights
full of sorrow as the soul
yearns for you endlessly.

In search for your love, the mind
has become tangled and twisted.
Will you ever know my thirst
for your ocean? The deep well
drowns the shallow soul and the
veil of mystery glows through
your mystical eyes. The moon
drapes your body with gray-silver
glow, and these eyes linger like dew-
drops on the delicate curves of your
form. Let the stars drift deeply into the
edge of night and burn away the
darkness of unfulfilled dreams. My
fate becomes trapped in the fullness
of her dark pearly eyes. Will

she ever fulfill life's only hope
as her steps burn on the surface
of my eyes. This smoldering
fire of existence arises from
the embers of her desires.
Dear love, you shed your scent
into the mystic air, and only
Nature can hold you against your
will. Will the night ever come to day
in love that sleeps under the glow
of twilight? Will you let the hand of the
drifting wind loosen the locks of your
silky black hair? Like a river searching
for its lost soul I run in search of your
love. In your days and nights, moments
of being no longer hold time. The
light washes away my darkness,
but in Divine love your spirit
grows sublime.

Love's Charm

In search of true love, you
come alive in dreams. It was
in love that God was created,
so it seems. The humble spirit
fans the flames. In your
heart you whisper her name.
Will you please send her
these flowers, so she can
make her bed of roses? Time
clings to hope that she will come,
but these trees stare at me in
their mocking poses. When will she
surrender her love and fall into
my arms? What happens to
longing that is lost in
mystical charm?

Silent Whisper

The unspoken words will shake
and tremble in our hands. Silence
pressed under our lips, like time
pressed into grains of sand. Life
is infinite shades of emotions the
world has never before imagined. The
tongue of humanity holds truth in silent
whisper that wisdom seldom fathoms.
Our eyes have become deep-rooted
in sorrow. The vision of life lifts us
to the sky, and there is much hope
in time borrowed. Will we seek
the wisdom that truth always
defends? We journey through
endless emotions in search of
our one true friend.

What will words say when they
fall in love with harmony of
sound? How will we be transformed
by reality when our words come
around? We shed our thoughts, and
our spirit reflects the words in our
heart. These words are heavy,
hard hitting, breaking life
apart. In total faith, words
will be written, but love will
make them true. Eyes have glanced
at them tenderly and the world was
made anew. Speak with
our inner voice and the spirit will
respond. Light has broken through
this heart of darkness, but true
love is nowhere to be found.

Deep-Rooted Tree

The silent tree has whispered to the
wind. Will you come into me to make
your eternal home? You have become
deep-rooted in life, and Earth is your
holy ground. Oh, children of this
world, play your games under my
shade. These branches beckon you
with alluring fingers as leaves spread
the sound of childhood laughter. I will
hold the sky above my shoulders, so
you can feel the warm summer breeze
touch your face. Will you sit under
my shade and reflect for a moment?

Let your spirit unwind as you lean
your back against my trunk. Please
don't be afraid as my bark will never
bite your tender soul. Will you listen
and slow your steps and not run so
fast? In my stubborn pride, I have not
walked for a hundred years. In many
storms I have been shaken, and the eyes of
the world have stared me down. The
winter's burden I have borne with
humility, but in your eyes, I am just
a tree. I can be your bed of dreams and
the roof of your existence. I can be
your burning fire in a world
that grows cold with age.

You come to me to cut me down, but I
wait for you with open arms. You leave
me with my burden so deep that I
shed my leaves totally broken-hearted.
I have become the tree that will grow
deep in your forest. In my lonely moments,
I have walked these mountains with heavy
steps. I have become the seed that will
grow into your human soul. Will you
let me bathe you in my light and wash
away your conscious existence? Will you
come toward me open-hearted? Your
slow steps are full of wisdom, and
have become deep-rooted in me. I
have become the living soul of
this world; touch me and
you will see.

Absolving Life

Somewhere in the honey dew
of spring butterflies dance in
their frenzy of colors captured
in nature's imagination.
From crevices of deep spirit,
light escapes through the
hands of the fluttering leaves
and creates your life song. How
fair are the tender eyes of the
night! The moon wanders like a
moth in search of the earth, its only
true love. The well has become
too deep to reflect your stillness.

In your shallow thirst the river
walks into your emotions, and
drowns your spirit. Will you give
up the ocean to breathe in the
salty air? The river branches into
your existence as you surface through
your watery abyss. Somewhere
the universe is round; it's neither
out nor in. Somewhere your voice
is calling; a flower is born inside
your rocky world. Will you seek
to touch its soul before it withers
and dies? Somewhere farther than
your dreams lurk the wandering
waves that walk on the sandy shores,
totally absorbed in their oneness.

Somewhere is the dark shadow of a
black-bird, resting on a tree, calling to
open your eyes to the morning light.

Somewhere, nature sleeps under the
veil of hidden beauty. Will you let
night's darkness open your eyes
to the light of a thousand stars?
Somewhere the mind reflects into
the body to comfort the soul.
Are we the dust of humanity in
dust to the greater whole?

The Boy Inside Man

These are the forgotten streets that
have held time still. Dissolved in
faded moments, my steps retrace the
moments etched in consciousness.
Youthful days bathed in splendor
echo from distant memories. In
dreams and reality these dark alleys
were the corridor of life's existence.
My hands no longer hold those
emotions of time in space. The spirit
was infinite then; the world held
infinite laughter. Houses now sit
motionless on concrete blocks,
staring at me with somber
faces, like strangers, looking
me over with fixed gaze. Through
their windows, I can feel the
soul of existence drain from me.

These were steep hills that my
legs struggled to climb. Here
the trees that were weak and
frail are now strong and tall. I
can still remember carrying my
heavy school bag, chasing my shadow
under the glare of the morning sun.
A mass of human flesh, full of noise
and hunger still gathers in school
cafeterias. After school's final hour,
I said farewell to friends, continuing

home alone. In freedom I yelled loudly
into the wind. My eyes searched
the sky, traced the path of fast-moving
clouds that led me home. There was so
much bliss in the world then; the
soul tickled one into joyful laughter.

Nights held so much mystery,
filled dreams with endless wonder.
Looking through my window I
could count a thousand stars,
always a few I counted twice.
What lay beyond those dark alleys
were vaporous shadows of timid youth.
The footsteps of my past, how fast and
quickly they ran! Now I walk through
them once more like a young
boy inside the man.

Reflection in Time

Will you lament time wasted
when all will be gone in time past?
We have become stagnant in the
will to move with time. How can
one come into being when he
lives in the past and fears
tomorrow? In his hands, the clock
holds still, as time breaks with
form, escaping through his
consciousness. A star ten billion light
years away is dead before it touches
your eyes. You are the dust in your
eternity and the wind can never
hold you within.

Time will come knocking at your
door to collect its dues with every
breath you take. The truth will grow
outward and mold your form in
moments of great reflection.
Under the immense sky, the mind
is eternal and unbound. Will you
walk to the very end of existence
and tell your story? Where do
the dead go when they are truly
dead in soul? Why shed tears that
will leave your spirit empty and
unfulfilled? We are born to live
and live to die for virtues that hold
no substance. You will die a thousand

deaths if you live empty in your
muted space. Will you look into
the mirrors of self-reflection and see
your face lined with age? Opaque
reality traps the spirit; the eyes
no longer see through the ground
glass of raw emotions. Will you wash
away your hard form in blackness
and come into light? Let the
mind heal your bleeding thoughts
as wisdom brings you to grace.

The heavy burden of the past
lingers in one's steps but he lets
the spirit walk free. In this
awareness, true words
surface, as one lets his emotions
sink deeply into his ocean. Will the
spirit hold silent thoughts in words?
Does one lament to the wind
when his life is the light inside
the burning flame? Those who
reflect in their beginning and
look toward their end know
whence life came.

Lost in Thought

In deep fragments of reality, the
sediment of experience settles to form
the layers of your being. Written
in your moments are thoughts that
have broken through the boundaries
of time. The urge to write and say
what one feels is no longer at hand.
The mind is restless, random,
and thoughts are no longer
bound to reason. Can one come
out of darkness to be captured
by light? How can one open his
eyes when he is still blind to truth?
In the stream of consciousness,
one escapes through his human form
to become one with his spiritual being.

Can one become a prisoner in
his new-found freedom? Is he
trapped in the maze of his own reality?
Let the echo run wild, and it will
come back to you totally changed. In
his spiritual home, the mind will
break the walls of sanity and create
a new perception of conscious will.
Fragments of life have come together
to make one whole. Can one gather
his form and become the mosaic of
his own existence? The human spirit is

the broken mirror of humanity
that still reflects one's
true substance.

True Reality

The fullness of youth is in the
life that we live. Can we rise
above our conscious reality and
breathe in the heavy burden of
being human? In our eyes we
have narrowed the sky, and
the world looks at us with an
unwelcome gaze. Can we lose our
existence to discover ourselves or
hold our conscious will to recover
ourselves? In this mix of fate,
our reality will never surrender
to the world. Moments of self-reflection
remain unmoved in our silent wisdom.
All will end, but then a new question
arises: why must all this come to
an end? Out of such quandary
heavens are born.

The end will be a new beginning
without end. In our darkest moments,
we will not reflect truth but reflect
only hard existence. How can one
have ideas that filter the mind's
certainty into the world? In the
will to move, time gives us direction
and the act of moving gives
momentum to the spirit. Can
the conscious eye take in the light
and awaken the mind to self-

realization? Why bow to tyranny
of needs and become a slave to such
desires? Does one know that his
craving for life has no salvation? Living
like this gives us no direction, as we have
no impulse to move, but move we
must, and that is what moves us
to remain. Why do we carry this
paradox of duality that pulls
us apart? Can we let our mind
engage in abstracts but speak
in concrete words? Human
nature blinds our senses as
our inner world reflects no light.

In our simple soul, true wisdom
will burn through our eyes and
become the spark of our new
beginning. Only true love will lift
the spirit, and free us from this
tangled existence. Our limit is reached,
but there are other limits within and
beyond these. Can we survive
in this finite existence when
infinity is all-encompassing? Can we
obtain the will to freedom and go
beyond ourselves? Our fate is like
waves of the ocean absorbed by the
sandy shores, never to move again. The
human spirit is like an actor who has
forgotten his lines and improvises in

the fear of being discovered. This is
space and time that linger like
shadows on a moment of luminance,
but will no longer exist once it has been
realized. The final thought is always
trailing closely behind almost within reach.
When the threshold is reached, the
peak of experience transforms us,
but only for a moment; then we sail
through the storm looking for the
reflection of a new beginning. Will
we run to the center of the storm
and let our whole world
go on spinning?

Fragile Rose

You are the bud in this
garden of roses. The wind
is the soul of a mother, and the
light a father's true love. Will
you sleep in tranquility and breathe
in your fragrance slowly and deeply?
Your world is born in this mix of
living colors; the beauty of
the world delights in your senses.
The universe is never whole until
your mind is one with it.

Move hand in hand with
time; hold it close to your heart.
Are we born too soon, only to
wither in our youthful ways?
Life is a gift that is given,
but it can be taken away at any
moment in time. Will you walk
away from these rays of hope and
turn your life into an illusion?
You have become a candle of the
night, and in your dreams, you toss and
turn on your humble bed. How much
thirst can you endure before you
drown in your own cup? How much
graceful dignity can you shed to this
world that holds no substance in grace?

Sweet is the water of the deeply-dug
well. How much reality do you hold
in your heart before stars settle
in your dreams? Will you surrender
your words against your tongue and hold
silence under the will of God? Walk away
from the burden of holding, and true love will
come into your heart. How will you touch the
sky with a spirit that is anchored to humanity?
Let emotions run in your veins and awaken
the heart in your essence first; become
rooted to earth before you can
walk on blessed ground.

You are mountains of scattered
dreams that will one day be broken
apart by the entropy of life. Oh,
Nature give your hands to creation
and shape the world in your majestic
poetry! Let there be no end to
your free will. The rose has been
plucked too soon, as the fragrance
bleeds into the wind. You are born
into the spirit of the living, and
in life you suffer for the
truth you can't find.

Lost in Life

Life was created in the essence of soul.
Like a mystical dewdrop that escaped
the awareness of the wandering
wind, we were born under the mist
of dawn. In the vastness of our
conscious eye, our life becomes
the spirit of reality and form.
The heart of nature runs
through our senses like a slow-
flowing river that carves into the
hard barren landscape. Let the
sensual breeze fan the flames of
passion and burn the spirit
into ashes of non-existence.

In hands of freedom, life will be
nurtured and molded in aged
wisdom. Let youth run free
into time, so we can grow strong
with age. God's vision is our sacred
truth, and the light is the bread for
the hungry soul. In every grain
of time, wisdom will collect and settle
in our mind. In slow moving steps, we
have journeyed far into life to come
back home to rest our weary spirit.

Will we cleanse the purity of spirit in the
water that we drink? A heart that reflects
in the transparent soul has neither walls nor

doors. We have washed away too many
sins in holy water. Why this great
thirst for the ocean when the shallow
river is all that is under our feet? Will
we forgive the mortal foe that gave
us great sorrow? What will become of
our being when death's hand closes
the door? In each moment of living,
we live and die seeking our purpose.
How will we take hold of the moment
that walks toward the sacred ground?
Nature has whispered in our ears that
life is coming to open our door,
but we are nowhere to
be found.

Etched in Time

In silence, you walk. The
wind comes and whispers in
your ear. Will you open your
heart to this world, let me in?
In true love, you will fulfill all
desires. Will you pick up the
pace and walk toward me? Life
comes and goes in full circle and
can never be broken. It will render
you brokenhearted before your
time. Will you seek joy in the
sorrow that cuts deeply? In
your deep laughter, you will
hear the echo call back to your
youth. Is it the mocking face
of time that reflects your light?

Is it the road that is winding too
quickly as your footsteps take you
into tomorrow? Open your eyes to the
world, and let the senses weave the
net into your spirit. You sleep and
dream among fields of daffodils. Is
there Heaven beyond the dome of the
deep blue sky? Will you unfold
your hands and let the butterflies
take flight on their joyous wings
of freedom? Let colors paint
your life on the canvas full of hope
and possibilities. With your artistic

brush, you create reality, and it
spills layers of infinite colors into
your conscious eye.

Your mind reflects the virtuous
vision of life that runs in
your blood. In the mirror
of your reflective soul, you are
once again broken by the rigid
reality of existence. Will you
open your doors and let life be a guest
for all eternity? A house that holds
wisdom warms the soul in its
walls of comfort. You have been
etched in time, as memories trace the
moments that felt sublime and all-
giving. Why do you walk away from
yourself before you near your end?
Let the soles of your feet journey
through time and give your shadow
the light to befriend. If you hear the
subtle laughter that life gives
you, then go no further than
your heart's content.

Of Being Human

We have suffered through our
humanity to become human again.
In our mind lives the voice of
self-destruction. There is no end
in our thirst for life, but in
our ocean the world holds folly
and exists surface deep. We have
become a prisoner to our own needs;
trapped and bound to our will like
mortality bound to humanity. Our
mind surfs on dreams that reality
holds from our consciousness.

Will we run into darkness with eyes
wide open? Why carry the baggage
of life when simplicity can lighten our
load and set us free? We are human,
but only humans setting fire to all that
we seek. In the vastness of existence,
we have become the carbon of life.
A speck of time for conscious living is all
that we are given. The human spirit suffers
from entropy, but the body will not set
it free. Where is the unity of wisdom
that gives face to human dignity? Why
don't we drink this wine of sorrow
from our bowl of happiness? A
thousand years of change, but we
still regress back in our evolution. Give
humans the light of eternity, and

they will waste it in no time. Are we
truly the creative spark in
God's imagination?

The human spirit burns with
the passion of being human, but
the noble soul will never let
that be. Will we open our
eyes to the will of being and
give wings to the spirit
that wills it to be free?

Hand and Soul

Will you give me your hand and walk
with me on this endless road toward
eternity? Let this unity take us far
into ourselves to become one with
our nature. A glimpse of light sparkles
in your gaze and comforts me in
hope for tomorrow. Will you let
me walk into your soul and find
refuge in your home? This
devotion to kindness is like a
stranger that you welcome at your
door. A heart that holds the hands
of sincerity is all that I seek.

What brings love into being? The
mind is deeply anchored to reason and
fails to open into human emotions.
Will you hold me in your arms
and let the sunshine burn your
form in my heart? In your presence
I have become the breath of conformity
that fades into the wind. The water
of reality runs deep in my blood, and
reflects the vision of divine love. A
spirit that grows in love gains
wings and yearns to touch the sky.

A soul that surrenders to the
faithful becomes human again.
A moment of empty silence is

all that we have become, as fragments
of sounds break away from our
inner being. Through the fragrance of life,
love grows and clings to the purity
of existence. Will you give this poor
soul the richness of your spirit?
The treasures of the world hold
no treasures greater than the treasures
of sheer existence. Did they not whisper
in your ear that the one you
seek lives inside of you? There is
so much that you will not see until
love has departed. True wisdom blinds
the human spirit, but love opens
the door and you walk in,
lighthearted.

Total Surrender

Why build fear in our
heart? A life that walks into
the path of existence breaks
through the barrier of time. A
spirit that holds no light to the
truth will drown its soul in the
gulf of darkness. How can we
wash away the ignorance that
stains our blood? Why do we
allow ourselves to get lost in
our ways of living? A stagnant soul
will find no road and give life no
path. Walk toward your shadow;
give your life the space it seeks.

Do we hold in our hands the
faith that we long to keep? A destined
path is realized once the will to move
pulls at our feet. The heart will love
the one who seeks the beauty of simple
existence. Will we let the colors of the
world grow in our eyes and become
the vision of our imagination? Hold
not the comforts of this world, but
breathe in the bliss of living. A life
saturated with emotions gives the
body no room and the spirit no home.

How will we reason with time that
escapes through our conscious will?

Why shed tears when perception rubs
deeply into our eyes? Why let go of
love that will never come our way
again, or whisper to nature the
love that we wish to find in us?
Let fire consume our
love and our will in
total surrender.

Reborn

What will they say when we
hold the heart of this world in
our dreams? Tear away your
flesh, and the comfort of reality
will find you warm clothes. In our
mind we remain hungry and seek
purpose, but our hearts still ache
for total acceptance. Where
are these lasting steps that walk
through life's journey and come
back to their very beginning.

We are born into the shadow of this
world, but only true light gives substance
to our bodily form. How much hope
brews under the depth of deep
sorrow? We shed empty tears
for wasted time and hope to
live further. There is no water
left to wash away the dust of
reality from our face. What
we will find in beauty is the soul
of God's creation. A thousand miles
we have marched to our destiny
but in every step, we yearn
to come home. Can we feel the
glory of being in every breath
we take? A strong hand
pulls us in and we unfold
under our youthful laughter.

We have come to live under
the vigilant sky as time runs
away from its moment of creation.
Can we bring back time, the
path toward life that has gone in
too deeply? A heart that drowns in
love is reborn in light of eternity.
We build our mind with walls of
wisdom that will hold truth strong.
Let the river hold our image in
its stream of consciousness and
humble our humanity with a
nod. What will we come to be
when we are created once more
by the loving hands of God?

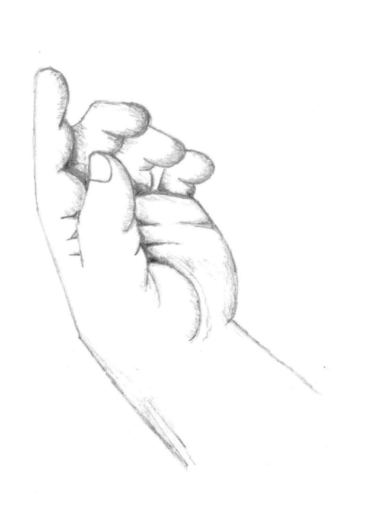

Hidden Treasures

In our endless search, we dig deep
looking for great treasures hidden
in our world. Only a blind soul digs
into themselves and struggles to look
for things that are no longer there. A
hand that tries to hold the wind comes
away empty-handed. A heart that
longs for love is not afraid of being
broken. The well of needs reflects no
bottom, but we will sink in our water
if we long to touch our reflection.
In thirst for glory, we become
a prisoner in seeking unending
pleasures; there is no room
for enlightenment.

Why tame desires when passion
rules with an iron will? Is our
true master the treasure we
seek? How deep is the river
of needs when all we can
drink is a handful of water?
The greatest treasures are
ours for the taking, but once
acquired, they are no longer ours.

A soul that lives for pleasure
dies of never-ending hunger. Lost
in blindness, we dig deeply into

earthly needs until they become
our grave. The ocean is the cup,
and our soul drinks, but in thirst
we have become its slave.

Will of Hope

The world will tumble and
turn against the axis of your
free will. Humans will live their
lives as if eternally ordained.
What can the spirit do but
breathe and give life its holy
mantle? Walk in pride,
and a speck of dust will
bring you down. Hold not
the wealth of this world but
the love that comes your way.

Walk in the footsteps of hope;
guard your being against the
rust of time. Will you pay your
debt to those who gave you
freedom without cause? Why
bargain with the piper and pay
a price that will be too steep? Like
a caged bird, your will has cut your
wings to freedom. There is no home
for the wandering soul lost on the
footsteps of never-ending journey.

Why not break away from all hope
and give your life a new name? Your
hands reach toward the sky to make
peace with the world. Why worry
about tomorrow when the wind
is so fair today? Your true

purpose in life is to savor
love before it is gone. Will you
fall in love today or long for
love that may never come
tomorrow? This world is a
dance of endless folly with
ever-changing reality of
hope and sorrow.

A Word Too Many

***

Those who judge others
become blind to the wisdom
of their reality.
The truth will judge you in your
deeds, and all other acts are lost
to sentimentality.

***

Let your determination point
the way, and your legs will
do all the walking.
In silence, you will hold your
tongue as your words will do
all the talking.

***

What the spirit needs is a candle
that burns at both ends.
Let your mind come out of hiding;
in light you will transcend.

***

In your moments of doubt, you will
fall with every step.
Will you walk in your humble ways as life
weaves its invisible web?

***

You can use force to oppress the people,
but you can't force them to
go against their will.
The human spirit is restless in freedom,
no power can hold it still.

***

The way of the masses is the
will of the strong.
If moral consciousness seeks the truth,
humanity can do no wrong.

***

If the will of the people speaks, then it
will lead to no slaughter.
It is better to appease your emotions
than to stir mud in water.

***

To work toward your success, you must give
it the love of your heart.
If you give it to those who never earned
it, they will tear it apart.

***

If you live your life in
deception,
you will be discovered in
self-reflection.

***

If you are rich on the backs of others,
fortune will carry you to
your grave.
In gluttony, you will hoard your
wealth; you have become its
master slave.

***

The price for true friendship will cost a
smile, a quick handshake.
Your only true friend always gives
but will seldom take.

***

The spirit of truth will lay bare the
light of your soul.
Break the walls of your consciousness to
become one with your whole.

***

Greed is like the ocean; if you jump
into it, you will surely drown.
Your health is your wealth, whether
you are king or clown.

***

A smile that hides the truth will often be
discovered on the wrinkles of
your face.
How will you face the truth that looks
at you without grace?

***

Those who hoard but never
give will one day lose themselves
in their hoarding.
In greed, you will thirst for
more and find it
never-ending.

***

If you are in debt, then
sell your home and walk
away debt free.
Only a fool will bargain for
more and go on a
spending spree.

***

The wealth that you build will one day
crumble with your last breath.
The only treasure worth keeping is the
one that strives for good health.

***

A borrower is like a gravedigger who
digs too deep and gets stuck in it for life.
How will you pay for your soul's
debt in the afterlife.

***

A life that is lived for the truth
will reflect your soul.
Your thirst will seek water as the
world will reflect in your bowl.

***

If a true friend walks deep into
your heart,
hold him close and never let him
depart.

***

A thousand days of living is
worth sacrificing for one
moment of true love.
In dreams time will hold
you eternally and elevate the
spirit to heaven above.

***

Steep is the ladder of success, but if you miss
a step, you will fall very quickly.
Those who succeed through failure
will see success clearly.

***

If you have no shame telling lies, then you will
truly be shameful telling the truth.
Those who are morally blind hold
no light in their youth.

***

The rich and the poor walk
on the same ground.
The rich suffer immensely in their pleasures,
but the poor make no sound.

***

How can you bargain with death? It can only
offer you a shallow grave.
A life that is sacrificed for the greater good
is truly noble and brave.

***

A jealous man will sneer and envy
the success of others.
He will make enemies among friends
and fail to grow any further.

***

Into the bowl of wine your spirit
will reflect through you to
reflect your whole.
Come, my friends, let the wine pour
into your thirst to liberate the
body from the soul.

***

Moments that burn deeply in
your consciousness, the heart
holds close at hand.

You have walked in the footsteps
of life as time is pressed
into every grain of sand.

***

The will to destroy is innately human.
Even the most civilized are sucked into
the lunacy of war.
Human passion holds no reason,
and blinded by power, it
doesn't see far.

***

The deeds of many years will be washed away
in one moment of anger.
Words that leave your mouth with contempt
touch the heart with a harsh clangor.

***

In your hypocrisy, your words will
hold no ground.
You have become a coward in your truth,
afraid of being found.

***

If you ask ignorance to sell
an intellectual thought,
then all words will lose their value
and can easily be bought.

***

Those who fear death often suffer immensely
in their moments of dying.
Have you lived life to the fullest in the heart's
final moments of sighing?

***

In the eye of a candle's light, the human
spirit will illuminate.
The body is but a burden under which
the spirit hibernates.

***

The entropy of life is in
flux of time, and no force
can keep you whole.
A life without a body is like a
spirit without a soul.

***

Each nation goes through
self-destruction through
which a new nation is born.
Truth will guide the masses when
the veil of ignorance is
raised and torn.

***

Oh, beauty, you have set the trap within my senses.
I have been captured, but my heart is full of sincerity.
Dear God, were you not in love with eternity?
I am a mere mortal; what are my chances?

***

When one fails, the spirit slips
into the depths of sorrow.
Wash away your pride and walk
toward your light. There is always
hope left for tomorrow.

***

If you judge others by your own
standards, a real judge will come

knocking at your door.
How will you see through your
duality in perception that is
no longer yours?

***

A criticism that is deflected
away from self often bounces
back fully reflected.

***

I am the water that moves deep
in your river.
Your thirst for existing reflects on
my surface, always and forever.

***

Shallow Waters

What voice is this that gave you
form? What is the impulse
that makes spirit strong? In
silence the world is bold
and full of emotions. Who is the
stranger that keeps knocking at
your door? Why do you fear the
darkness that opens your eyes?

In true strength, you will find
true weakness. You seek
pleasures of this world, but
lose them in moments of seeking.
In total faith, the soul finds great
comfort in sorrow. In search
for direction, you come to know
that you are all, and all is within what
you seek. How can infinity define
consciousness of human reality?
In your beginning and end there
is only one time for true living.

You have become non-existent
in the vastness of your universe.
Will you lighten your wisdom by
weighing the burden of ignorance?
In depth of your spirit, you will find
your craving for existence. Your true
self is like a river searching for the
greater truth. Will you look into
your being fully reflected
in part and in whole? A shallow
life is not worth living
when you are seeking the
deeper soul.

Open Your Door

In our wonder, we take in
the world with fullness of
laughter. Will we let reality bind
our faith and imprison us in our own
eyes? In our moment of awareness,
time is born to hold us in all moments.
A dream that gives way to the sentiments
of the night casts a net of luminance
for the dawn of day.

In the beginning life set the
trap, and one' faith became a web
of illusion. How will the body overcome
harsh reality, as the soul searches
for eternal truth? The mind seeks
the will to be, but conscious
existence has washed it away.
Only a translucent soul breathes
through the purity of water.

How will we face our virtues
that lay naked the moral truth
of being human? A thousand
times we will grow old in a life
tarnished by the world. Let us
humble our pride, lighten our feet,
and the inner-voice will walk us
toward life's journey. Will we silence
our heart of envy to give true love its
eternal home? The doors to life

have opened, and we have willed
ourselves to be our own guest.

Only through hardship can we
truly gain wealth of happiness.
Will we take the lesser road to break
free from the hands of conformity?
Like beads on strings, moments
of pure joy roll from the fingers with
no strings attached. Come into
yourself like a guest and let there
be no other. We are bound to
taste reality like sweet wine bound to
water. The destiny of our path is
far and near. Why break away from
our inner circle? This life is full of
wisdom and has called for us
to come out of our door. Will
we not listen to the truth
of all truth before the
silent whisper is no more?

Watered Truth

What falls before our eyes is
the pure light of existence. Will we
lift the veil of mystery and let our
true love be known? What becomes
of the wind when life breathes in
the spirit of being? We shed tears
through our laughter, but in sorrow
we make them run too fast. Why
not wash away the ashes of our reality
in our holy water of certainty? A
wandering mystic searches for true
love in a soul that has no dwelling.

Will we use clay to build our form
in a world that holds no substance?
How can the mind mold certainty
when consciousness slips through
fingers of awareness? Oh, aged wisdom,
nature has seduced our will, and there
is stagnation in our mortal steps. In
love of beauty, we have surrendered
our hearts, but a prisoner to desire
we shall never be. We have
set our souls afire; and
it consumes the senses whole. Will
we come into our light of existence
and wash down the dust of
creation? Let the river walk into
our ocean and drown us in

our narrow ways. Silence breaks
through these words as watered
truth cleanses night into day.

Body in Form

The wind has walked in quietly
and whispers what we long
to hear. We have built our home
beyond walls of freedom, but
still our doors are sealed. The
will to live still holds us prisoner
under the veil of temptation.
That which is lost too quickly our
hearts savor with eternal desires.

The mind grasps firmly the
spirit that leads us toward truth.
How deeply must we breathe
to awaken our soul? Just close
your eyes. Let nature's breeze touch
the senses and spill into your emotions.
Can consciousness be born in a mind
that drowns in uncertainty? Will we
let love break our hearts to give life
its everlasting sorrow? In body and
form, light will reflect into the
mirrors of the great soul. Will there
be unity of spirit when the walls of
reality are finally broken? Our eyes
will not hold light of reason
until we overcome all reason.

How can we find peace when our
spirit is broken by our world of
deception? Why burden the mind with

intellect when the rational soul
holds no thought? Flesh ages
and slackens the body, but our
spirit remains firm in our simple
ways. The wind calls our name,
"unshoulder your burden; breathe
in the open air." We have become
the dust of human creation, unsettled,
pulled down by time's heavy
hand. The mind's eye opens
into the dreams of night as the
body dwindles and sleeps.
Hands that strive to create
are the same hands that strive to
destroy creativity. Existence will
hunger always if hunger remains
deep. Life's calm moments will echo
and settle in our youthful form,
but in all other moments
we will have to weather our
conscious storm.

Light Minded

Will we let light awaken our
mind and burn into our world
the fragrance of existence? The
light has come strong and fast
to bring us closer to the secrets of
the universe. Oh, light! What is the
impulse that moves you far and
wide? How do you spread your
colors on the canvas of this world?

In eyes of total darkness your
love is deep, your embraces
warm and bright. The story of the
past you bring with calm awareness.
In light of truth, you make the
world all-knowing, all-revealing. In
the strong pull of time and space, you
escape through the twisted snare of
reality. In your vastness you
are battered, bruised, and bent,
but you journey endlessly to come
home to humanity. Light sprinkles
and paints nature with infinite
colors, weaving the garment of
divine creation. Look through
the veil of enlightenment and
give life its fleeting moment
of wisdom.

What becomes of light when its
fragmented nature becomes whole?
You are born light-minded but in your
soul, you are still light years in
becoming. What happens if one runs
faster than light? Let light
cut through the dark world
and glow in luminous
splendor. Oh, light, will you
illuminate the hope of all living
things and give our eyes your
conscious vision? Will you come
into our ocean of darkness
and wash away all doubts
and illusions?

Call to the Wind

The echo of our voice reaches
deep into existence, awakening
the spirit to take in the moment.
Have we become the mystical drop
that falls onto the surface of reality,
creating ripples in our conscious
river? We have become the circle in
our whirling dance where there
is no center of realization. We
breathe in our youth, strong and
expectant. With age, wisdom
ripens the soul, and true beauty
surfaces. Nature calls the wind to
come out and play in the valleys of
our exposed landscape. An invisible
hand stirs the senses, the world
rises in a symphony of music, as
we crave with reverence the voice
that whispers our name. Innocence
is the child inside the man; true
love will bind them as one. This
whirlwind will not hold us straight, but
will pull us in, even against our will.

We call the wind to speak of this
silent mourning pressed under our lips.
The heaven we seek is here, now;
there is no other heaven worth seeking.
Why hold things that give no pleasure
when life gives so much in abundance?

In humble moments, we are awakened
in light; our spirit is washed in faith
and hope. Only a tender soul can
touch a lover's heart and free
the spirit to live its days. A life that
submits to the will of time gives
birth to the seeds of all creation.
In the candle of our eyes, love
holds all form and will burn away the
darkness of our world. Beauty
glows and warms the emotions in our
heart and melts the coldness of reality.
Why do our sentiments thirstily
smolder for our being? Our life is a
fragment of a thousand dreams under
the sun, but we still search for golden
light. This one moment in time will
bring us into the eyes of eternity;
to be forever etched in time,
keeping us forever young. Oh
youth, we grow old too quickly.
Point your finger at time;
there lies the blame. We
will become dust in dust,
whence once we came.

In the sound of our laughter, life
fills with joy that spreads out into
the wind, awakening the world's
eye at dawn. What will be the fate
of humanity when humans become

less human? For those we love, will
we weep handful of tears to comfort
their sorrow, and hold them in our
smile and laughter? The north
wind will stir the waves; dreams
will soak into our sandy shores.
In boundless vision, all becomes all,
and no one thing opens us deeper
than the one we love. Frozen in our
hearts is the certainty that only
time will reveal the sweet desire
that feeds the ravenous soul.

Will you go and tell the
wind that she is coming? Her
fragrance spreads into the air
and comes knocking at nature's
door. Love is bound to eternity
as we fade into it
evermore.

Call to Faith

We give in to our faith totally
as we surrender our will
to God. Why do we grieve in
sorrow for the living when divine
destiny will take us far on our infinite
journey? Let the wind walk through this
rose garden in full splendor. We are
born to the fate of being trapped
in the noose of our own making.
The infinite soul never hungers for
the comfort and wealth of this world.

Should one beg for eternal
existence when this one moment is so
full of eternity? Will we drink from
the bowl of wisdom to quell our
thirst for realization? There is so
much life that will reflect our
light. Shall we weave life's web so
we can become entrapped in
our reality? Only a fool chasing
the wind attempts to grasp it.

Why hold ourselves underwater
and call it home? Open
your eyes to the beauty of this
world, to see your true purpose.
If we are bound to our shadow,
then we hold no light in our
form. Nothing remains in

emptiness but emptiness itself.
The will to be free catches us
breaking away from our destined
path. Then, in the need to reason,
we will find no reason to seek
the truth. What is the path to
Heaven that our faith must take?

Life ends in its beginning when
the end moves towards us. Our
will to live is forever seeking
more time. How will we reclaim
time wasted on empty dreams? A
speck of dust is all of humanity,
and life will not overcome its
mortality. There will be no moral
virtue in a faith that becomes blind.
We would be outsiders to our
inner faith if we make too
much fuss. We must open
our heart's door
and call to faith
to join us.

Enemy of Youth

Oh, youth! Did you not polish
Alexander's mirror to reflect
our destined path? Buried in the
moment is the revelation of our
eternal ways. Let the summer
breeze stir our emotions and soften
our hearts. The nightingale's
song captures the wind, and
the delight of nature dances
in the mystical night.

Let the rose burn in ashes of
deep red hue, as the sweet fragrance
awakens the conscious eye of the
sleepy wind. Shall we bestow on
our true love the pleasure of
life? We are destined to walk
into tomorrow, but it is our
spirit that pulls us back to
our beginning. Can we ever
bargain with fate to regain time
that runs fast in our pulses? Did it
not occur to Yusuf that youth would
rekindle the heart of Zulaikha once
light unveiled the mystery of love?
Oh, beloved! Let me drink the water
that reflects your soul and drown of
thirst in your ocean a thousand times.
You have become a prisoner of your
own making; no resolve can set

you free. In your dark, pearly eyes the
world is consumed into non-existence.
Oh, beauty, the will has surrendered, but
fresh wounds still burn under the skin.
How will you pour the ocean into a cup
that holds no water? Why would you let
love walk away broken-hearted, unfulfilled?
Though time becomes youth's enemy, love
ripens it with age. Oh, youth! Life has
come and gone too quickly; no human
can gain. In one instant of love, all
was light, but now only shadows
remain.

Hands of Serenity

A life that is born in wonder
lives and grows in wonder.
A passionate soul sets fire to the
conscious mind and awakens
it beyond all limits. Who
among us has truly opened his
heart to the beauty of the world?
What can nature be but a gift
to the senses, distilled in purity
of time and space? Shall we follow
the path home to begin anew?
Our existence is a moment of
joining two ends to become
one. Our destiny is to live
completely in our moments.

Just bring it full circle. The
child breaks through the empty
shell of man to crawl out into a
world of freedom. Will youthful
pride ever bow to old aged
wisdom? One's body becomes
the continuous burden, but our
soul must overcome this burden
of life. A life full of curiosity
seeks beyond the meaning
of existence. At birth, one becomes
a guest of this world and to
no avail, for the restless
spirit has no home.

Only a fool chase unfulfilled
desires, allowing time to escape
through their conscious will.
Give others what you would give
yourself in abundance: a spirit
totally absorbed gives light
to wisdom and approaches
self-awareness. The heart beats
with serenity; the mystical voice
calls you to express your deep faith.
Will your steps take the homeward
path? Have you walked through
life with humbled pride? In
harmony, the fullness of self
has a firm hold on reality. Hands
of serenity have molded you with
love, an ageless spirit
beyond mortality.

The Gift of Love

The gift of love becomes rooted
in the soul. One who gives
shall find fulfillment in all
he has given. The heart of the
beloved is radiant, made of
soft gold. How can one protect
the precious from the world's
envious eyes? One's spirit
wanders, but she is the light
that guides this endless journey.
In the dimness of night, the silent
wind slumbers under the shadow of
her dreams. From the depths of
her ocean one can never reach
the shallows. Creation grows
out of emotions as we search
for true love. Stars glow in
our eyes, the light of eternal
longing. Will we burn in our
tears, lamenting the beauty of her
true form? A lover holds delight
in arms that surrender to the
will of passion. In her world the
soul finds an everlasting home.

Life has folded into the twilight
of forgotten dreams. Her beauty has
awakened the senses and etched her
perception deep into the core of
reality. The forest has stirred the

wind and the trees shed her fragrance
into the sensuous breeze. The gift
of soul is love's only bargain and
life desires naught else. Dear
beloved, you are still smoldering
in the ashes of creation as smoke rubs
your beauty into these misty eyes.
What will be the world to you
in love that never dies?

Embers of Passion

Her face reflects the beauty of
heaven and binds her to light.
The softness of her hands is like
silk that comforts the jagged soul
and keeps the body warm. In her calm
stillness, she stirs the loving summer
breeze that sounds the sweet melody
of her being. How can one escape the
mystical pull that beckons him in with
it's tantalizing, seductive charm?

Like a red rose colored with the
vigor of freshness, she is the image
of divine beauty. The fate of true love
has plucked the rose before its time
and nature bows to the hand that
takes it with pleasure. It is the eternal
yearning in a lover's eyes that sparkles
with the light of a thousand stars. If
dreams escape through the everlasting
night, reality will never awaken the
conscious soul. Will we live in fragments
of time and seek the moment that
binds us to truth? A love that is blind
is an illusion of true love and lacks
heavenly grace. In the depth of
her beauty, the heart is shallow, but
passion remains heavy and strong.

What will be my fate when she looks my
way and takes me in? Oh, wind of fire!
Please burn through the forest;
let no tree escape her burning
soul. Let me become her ashes.
Scattered through the night by an
unforgiving wind, there will be no hope
for unity. Will rain ever extinguish
these red-hot embers as desires
burn and smolder through this
smoke-filled destiny? Let me
drink the water of being from
her cupped hands. Dear
beloved, if you fill this cup a
thousand times I will thirst for
a thousand more. How far
must one wander, how deep
must he look into life
for love that is
evermore?

Lost Time

Shall we listen to our moments
of silence? Life imparts its
truth. Youth calls our name
in a world that is lost in time.
Listen to the sweet voice of
reason, as echoes from the
past call us to receive life's
only wisdom. A child is the only
delicate flower of this world that
blossoms, giving hope to
the human spirit.

Youth is the river that flows
gently through our consciousness
in search of great oceans. Who
is the keeper of time as age falls
at our feet? Shall we embrace
the world in our journey, as we
search for truth with each step?
A hundred years of life is but
a fleeting moment when we run
through it with no purpose. Why
do we lose ourselves in search of
eternity? Oh, youth! You have come
and gone with such swift vigor that your
splendor still lingers in aftertaste!

Faded moments of the past remain to
carry our name to the end of time.
Will our inner-eye recall bygone

days as youthful laughter followed
us on our never-ending road? Will we
let wisdom settle into the sediments
of knowledge? Man will shed
his human nature to let the child
grow in his heart. Deep in our
spirit is the will to freedom that
no longer carries the burden of
existence. What is man but a blind
soul lost in the world's senses?
Let our spirit breathe in fresh
air, and give the mind a moment
to reflect. How will we hold the
weight of fate when youth breaks
from time, and wisdom mocks
free will? Let us mirror our
humbled faces, reflecting the
light into our past. In youth time
never caught us at our game,
but in old age it has
found us at last.

A Word Too Many

***

A life lived in greed
will always fear poverty.
The riches of this world will
make you poor if you don't give
them with generosity.

***

One who deceives others may gain
for the moment,
but one who deceives himself
finds no atonement.

***

Can one satisfy greed if one
gives in to it day and night?
If ever one can see the well of evil,
there will be darkness, no light.

***

Who among you has the gift
of giving?
Who among you has the will
of living?

***

A man who holds no purpose, stumbles
on his path of existence,
lost in the ways of the world, walks
far, but covers no distance.

***

If you walk toward your blindness,
you surely will hit a
dead end.

Life is never a straight road; there
are turns and unexpected
bends.

***

Those who oppress others are often
oppressed by their consciousness.
There is no joy in power that robs
others of their happiness.

***

In the stream of time, the present, past,
and future are what make life whole,
but there is no life in living until one
makes peace with mind, body, and soul.

***

Time is the product of consciousness;
no consciousness, no time.
Can you invest in these moments
your nickels and dimes?

***

Our shortcomings will fan
the flames of jealousy.
Why hold anger that will
become our enemy?

***

A life that is wasted chasing dreams
will put us in our grave.
Only a fool bargains with death and
becomes Satan's slave.

***

Those who fall but rise again
use care to never fall again.
Success that strives for success
and happiness is never in vain.

***

We are guests of this world; live in
peace to your very end.
Love will hold us strong among our
enemies and friends.

***

A mountain of dreams lives
inside the man, only to chase
the tail of fortune to no end.
Greed will grind our needs
to the core until our lives
are fully spent.

***

The measure of intelligence is to
realize how little you know.
Humility is born inside the
child, but in man it ceases
to grow.

***

One who seeks has the will and hope
to know. Seeking to know is the
act of it being known.
Will our eyes recognize the face
of truth in light that our
wisdom has shown?

***

Simplicity is the product of
complexity; one must simply
come to terms with it.
Humility can open many doors
to knowledge, but to enter one
must be morally fit.

***

A doctor who knows too
much can be malignant to
his patients.
The art of healing is to exhaust
one's limitations.

***

Happiness comes in circles; hold onto
it the next time it comes around.
The joy of living comes and goes, but
only in true love can it be found.

***

Women are form;
men are shadow; light
is the only dividing element.
The world will see with worldly
eyes, but filters with
infinite sentiments.

***

It is often said that true love
is blind; just open your eyes,
and see for yourself.
If true love is ever found, it
will bind you forever
to someone else.

***

Seek and you shall find. Look in
all directions, but never behind.
See and you shall know. Walk in
silence and let your thoughts
go. This world is your soul; open
your heart and see. Live your life in
the moment; what shall be, shall be.

***

What are these tears in your eyes
but the joy that weeps for hope
that never dies?

***

What is in life that you live
but the joy in sorrow that it gives.

***

The body is to the soul,
a mosaic of truth to
the spirit whole.

***

What is in a face
but God's spirit in
human grace.

***

What is darkness to light
but a vision of day to dream
into night.

***

What is truth
in love
but a path to Heaven
above.

***

The seeds of reality have been
sown into the spirit of
the mind.
Bear the fruit of your
awareness by seeking truth in
what others find.

***

Moral virtue is as vast as the universe,
but its act is no bigger than the
human heart.
Life may be lived in all goodness,
but only our deeds are what
sets us apart.

***

Wise are those who cherish
what they hold.
Ignorant are those who
cherish what they
have sold.

***

What is your destiny to
your fate
but steps to wisdom that come
home late.

***

Happiness is the poverty of joy;
the richness of life, the rich
find ways to destroy.
Your eyes reflect the light
of the wandering moon.
Walk away from this heart of
darkness come home soon.

***

Memories

Memories fly in the sky like butterflies in
the open breeze;
silent dreams breaking through the night only
the inner-eye can see.
Half-forgotten moments etched into playful days
pressed on the sands of time,
as childhood wisdom grows into the human voice
like a playful melody in rhythm and rhyme.
In love we were born; so much love is in our hearts.
How much life have we spent in moments
of reflection to give our spirit a head start?
On our journey, we walk endlessly to
bring home words of wisdom.
Our conscious will shall hold its breath as
memories reflect the light in our vision.
Dust settles in our soul, the joy of
living shines in our eyes,
smile as memory brings life full
circle of years gone by.

Mystical Dreams

Will you come into the caves of
my dreams and give me the night
to sleep under your existence?
Oh, beloved, you are born in these
mystical emotions, and my eyes
have given you form. The night is
filled with silence, the stars flicker
like jewels and cling to sky's black silk
gown. I can hear the wind knocking
at my door, whispering your name.

Will you come into my senses and
spread your light in this heart full
of darkness? The wide-eyed moon reflects
her light as her soul casts shades of worldly
sentiments. Her fragrance has embraced
the wind and awakened the spirit of
nature. She has sown the seeds of poetic
vision in body and form. In the cold
embers of red-orange glow heave
the desires of infinite longing. She
warms the spirit that blankets
life in the coldness of humanity.

In her presence, I have become
wandering dust, hoping to settle at
her feet. Let the softness of her body
sweeten the redness of these tender
lips. Give me one moment in time to
see her face, etched in my memory.

In my tossing and turning, the
strong heart aches and calls her
name. When will she come and
fill this cup of destiny? Dawn's
hand parts the veil of mystery
from her eyes, but is it dream
or reality I seek in her?
Awakened in my eyes are desires
to search for her in a world
I once knew. Dreaming
a thousand dreams are worth
chasing when the one
you love is a dream
come true.

Hindered Light

Your heart is like a river
running on the surface
of my soul. In love you
shall breathe in the depths
of your ocean, but unfulfilled
thirst is all you crave.
The union of one love is
never two. The beloved
reflects in me, but water is
her true-life source. When
light pours into the spirit of
her eyes, she is born in divine
perfection. What one sees
in pure darkness are the eyes
that reveal her beauty. Why
do the blind look for love
in all the wrong places?

You walk tirelessly all day in
tattered clothes, like a nomad
looking for the rose in your
desert garden. Do you not
know that the one you seek is
inside you, glowing with
white golden light? The world is
in rhythm with her heart, and
seeds of consciousness have
taken root in her existence.
If I whisper her name, the
hands of the wind will arouse

rapturous joy in fields of
colorful roses. The fragrance
of her spirit is like jasmine
opening its soul in the stillness
of night. Beauty is eternal
and yet so quickly withers
and wrinkles with time. Under
the mercy of her will, time
will abandon us and the
empty heart will be broken
forevermore.

Why do you burn flesh of
hope from your spirit when there
is no chance of her coming?
These eyes falter at death's door,
somber and bewildered when I
can find her nowhere. I
hear her mocking my
helplessness
as I lay trapped in
my delusions. Oh Hafiz!
Will you give me the wisdom
of your Divan and let her
come in as my soul burns?
Dear Lord, please don't
let light hinder her
beauty for which this
heart yearns.

Future Behold

The mask of reality sustains
the face of human folly.
A spirit slows to stagnation when
fear grows beyond the will to exist.
The present rests in your hands,
but the future is light years in
the making. Who is the stranger
who, without knocking, walks in
uninvited? Under the dirt of your
feet, the intellectual mind collects
the sediment of knowledge.
Can you speak truth and
let words of wisdom escape
through conscious lies? You have
become the echo in the wind, and
wings have lifted your kindred
spirit. Will you break your
silence with the world, to
live silently in your heart?

Can words hold sound without
truth of wisdom? Can one
wash away all meaning that is
stained with the blood of humanity?
The secret of life's purpose is to
live inside a mystic's heart. When
one finds truth in full light, the
revelation of wisdom is clear.

True beauty hides behind the veil
of mystery; once discovered it
permeates the longing heart.

Sweeten the wine to give joy to
this thirsty cup. What will become
of wine when water dilutes your
senses? How can true love
exist without a spark from
love itself? Hidden under this
mask of reality is the beauty
you have purled. Only an
awakened soul breathes in
the freshness of morning
light and sheds the body
from the world.

Self-Reflection

Thou art the mirror of
self-reflection that looks
in all directions for self-
realization. What brings
us forth is the divine
light of God's existence.
How will we come to
terms with our awareness
of non-existence? Look into
our own mirrored eyes and
let light open the doors
to our darkness.

Can we break away from
the shadow clinging to our
spirit? How far will our
thoughts sink before they touch
the depth of our unconscious
will? A life that moves with time
journeys to its very end and
scatters with entropy. We
are all infinite colors
of many shades dissolved
in the water of pure emotion.

What will be our true nature
when reason erases the lines
of our form? Humanity holds
our spirit naked, but humility
clothes us with self-perception.

There will be unity in our
wisdom when experience
bridges the gap between body
and soul. Let the two universes
become one, and there will
be no need to seek oneness.
Divine spirit is deep ocean,
and one is the drop of water
striving to become whole.
The roundness of self-reflection
will touch our surface and
rest calmly in our bowl.

Spring Awakens

In the eyes of spring's first
awakening sleep the seeds
of a lover's dream. Let the
rains come; let them open
life's full potential and
awaken eternity from
its deep slumber. Dawn
settles in misty dew.
Blades of grass are damp
and humble, and joyous
daffodils seduce the senses
with seductive poses.

Hummingbirds flip-flop
their wings in jubilation,
licking the nectar of flowers
with bleeding hearts. The eye is
set in perfect harmony as nature
plays under the glorious light of
the golden sun. We hear the
blissful sound of oncoming birds
that fill the sky with all their glory
as trees proudly spread their
branches to shoulder them on
their long journey home. A slumbering
whisper to the cocoon and metamorphosis
gives wings that break open to touch the
sky. A warm gust of wind takes hold
of moving butterflies; colorful wings

cut into the breeze, dance, swing,
and sway in their drunken state.

Sweeten the soul with honey that
pours into our being from
nature's bowl. Fall in love with
the open fields, as we run from
the world, totally absorbed.
The coming of spring has
finally broken winter's will.
Open the windows; come out
into the majestic world, see
the colors scattered by light.
Hear the heart's laughter,
as spring's warmth and
daylight banishes the
dark will of night.

Wisdom Behold

True wisdom is nameless, and
holds no reality. Like the wind, it
assumes no direction but walks into
the soul when the heart's doors unlock.
Wisdom holds nothing sacred but
gives back to the world all that we
fail to give. We shall be consumed
by fate and time will mold us into
rigid reality. Can we gaze into our
own eyes and reflect into the deep
well of spirit? Will we break through
our silence to let the will speak
truth of true existence?

If we awaken in the moment and
breathe, the world will bear our heart
to devotion. We are deeply-rooted in
our native blood, but our thirst will
consume the water of our souls. We
learn to walk on the surface of reality,
but it is the weight of our emotions that
holds our feet firmly to the ground. In the
mirror of our own eyes, we reflect
awareness, but what we see
reflects no light.

The great love of nature sustains all
creation. The boundless soul is whole in the
oneness of the universe, conscious in every
fragment of the whole. Let go of desires

for greatness and share humility with
the world of humanity. Those who
are rich in spirit suffer not in their
humble existence. Will we recognize
wisdom when it comes walking along
our path? Once there is steadiness and
unity in all things, wisdom will find us.
The human spirit will burn the house
and destroy the walls of vanity.
This journey into life's vast
realm breaks away
from the will to
immortality.

Burning Faith

When we first met, life's
true purpose was realized.
Like a river's eternal longing,
your spirit poured into mine
to become the deep-sea of true
love. You are the only reality
that builds no walls, no boundaries.
Nature's deep secrets are rooted in
divine wisdom and revelation of truth
nurtures and grows unbroken. The
mind opens the doors to Creation
and light emanates with luminance.

Human nature lingers in darkness,
but hope is still the light we come
to see. What is the great substance
that clings to and embraces our
unworldly dust? What can light
give our spirit but a shadow that
carves out the limits of reality?
How will our heart absorb this
sacred love for life? In the caves
of eternal spirit, flames of passion are
etched on walls of stone. Our souls
reach for each other; but time alone
can bind us together as one. How can
absolute purity wash the tinges from
human creation, thou asketh? Dear
Lord, there is no god but God,

and what God You shall be
glows in the embers of our
burning faith.

Life's Essence

What is the essence that
makes one human? What
is the garment that hides
true nature? Our spirit
is the essence that washes up
on the shore and awakens
us into our true-life form. How
can we love when our essence
cuts into the unity of whole?

Flesh is the mask that hides
true beauty. The mystical
eye sees hidden truth in
flesh and bones. Shall we
let our unspoken words
become reality? If we
speak quietly, our words will
gain a voice. The secret of
all that is beautiful is in the
eyes that behold the splendor
of beauty. A blind soul walks
through darkness of this
world and looks for the wicked
in all that is good. What is true
in life is the joy of living another
day. A tinge of color and a spark
of passion shatter the glass walls
of our transparent soul. What
defines us is our humanity
that we uncloak from pride.

The face that comes into being is
the one we see on the surface
of self-reflection. Drink the
substance of life from our bowl
of existence. The stillness of
water in the depth of the
human spirit holds too
much residue, too much
truth. So, we shall let it
become the wings of our
imagination to lift us
above our youth.

Good and Evil

Evil walks into an idle soul
when the doors to our soul
are left open. Evil seeks the
the weak soul and tries to
blind us with darkness of
our immoral will. A foolish
spirit that thirsts for power
will never see the true power
of evil. Wisdom sheds light
into the darkness of evil and
will never surrender its truth.
Violent passions are the ashes
of reason when evil burns
the mind with no self-control.

Good and evil look the
same when the soul lives in
self-decay. True evil takes hold,
when fear gains control of our
emotions. A weak mind will be
bent and conquered by the will of
evil. Those who oppress the free
spirit often oppress their own will
to be free. Those who envy power
and hold it fast become
powerless and unfulfilled. Evil
will trap the soul of humanity
and help us dig our own
grave. The stench of evil that

burns through the air will suffocate
the masses. The presence of evil is
weakness in our morality, destroying
the mind of human reasoning.

True evil causes the destruction
of soul, leading to great suffering.
The root of all evil is ingrained
in human passion that is empty
of spirit and savage to all that
is virtuous in this world. Good
and evil are the footpaths of
humanity, pressed in every
grain of sand. To evade
evil, we must keep great
good close at hand.

Self-Reality

An unmoved mind sits in the
forest and moves all things around
without itself being moved. The
spirit is born empty, growing
into consciousness, becoming
the water in our great ocean. A
mindful spirit listens in silence,
hearing the mysterious universe in
total awareness. In our infinite void,
we hold nothing of value and bear
no seeds of evil. The mind avoids all
chaos when the tranquility of wisdom
walks on surface of time and space.

Truth will shed light, giving
humanity no anchor to
darkness. Eyes reveal only
what eyes wish to see. Why don't
we become pillars of reality
and let our burdens be lifted?
Let the mind wander freely on
consciousness of our intellectual
journey and bring us back
fully transformed.

If we let the spirit pull us in, our
will to be will self-implode. Grasp
time by your hands; hold it for one
moment of self-realization. In
one moment we exist, but in

the next we are unrealized. The
soul lives in non-existence, but
gives spirit to the existing body.
Have we lived reality, accepting
the fate our will approves? The
mind wonders and ponders in the
enormity of thought and walks
away unmoved.

Bridge to Reality

Where is this eye of reality
that lets us see our created
being? Will we be conscious of
the light that comes from distant
stars? Shatter the human form
into a thousand pieces, and our
true self remains one with every
piece. The voice of nature melts
the words of time and the spirit
rests in silent truths. What is
the substance that sustains the
universe? What is the hand that
moves the conscious will?
The silk of reality's web is
the only line of hope for the
human spirit. So why does the
soul struggle in deception of
its own making?

Our will is our prison; no
will can set us free. Behind this
beginning is a new beginning
and beyond our end, we will find
no beginning. A mind full of
wisdom knows all paths to
mindful living. A life lived
for others fills with each
moment of living. What is
the true essence that runs
deep within us? Measure

the truth in every reflection
of light that touches our eyes;
just as a river seeks the
ocean from shallow ground,
the soul seeks out the
body, but only in true love
will it ever be found.

Lying Soul

What happens to morality
when faced with hypocrisy? Only
a coward hides within himself,
afraid to look into the mirror
of his inner truth. Words are
powerless when they fall on
deaf ears. True virtue is born
through deeds and becomes the
moral ground for conscious living.
How does one come to terms with
light of truth that glows dimly in the
darkened world? If one listens to
his thoughts, moral truth will
echo in his conscious soul.
Let truth burn in our passion,
and consume our simple
will. How else can we
deal with our human will?

The world is the fruit of human needs;
no sweetness can fulfill the hungry
soul. In life, we are born to walk
in our moral truth, but suffer
in moments of human duality.
Let these sediments of certainty
settle beneath the moral virtue of
our consciousness. If greed
consumes us, there will be
no air left to breathe in
happiness.

The spirit is without substance
when morality escapes the mind,
and the soul can no longer bring it
back. We hears taunting laughter,
but we ignore it mockingly. When
hypocrisy overcomes reason,
virtue will never succeed;
the moral and ethical
thing to do is to tear down
the walls of lies until
the soul is freed.

Hidden Truth

Can true knowledge give our
form the depth of reality? Filter your
mind through your conscious eye
and the mold of experience will line
your face. What is knowledge but the
will that hides the truth, the reality that
stirs the senses, and the mind that
makes it all-knowing? To seek is
to strive toward truth; seeking
to know will make it complete.

True wisdom never holds our hands
against time, but opens our doors
to the world of all its mysteries. A
curious mind is the light inside the spirit
of man, and lives outside the boundaries
of rituals and beliefs. The hidden
genius lives inside the soul of humanity,
but only curiosity can move it
toward greatness. The thirst for
truth takes us on a journey, giving
us the ability to reach beyond the
boundary of self. If we endure life's
trials, the mind will become a universe of
wonder. How deeply shall we immerse
ourselves in the quest for true
meaning? Only humility can
humble us in our wisdom.

The more we seek, the less we know.
Eternal truth rests with eternal time;
no civilization will bear the whole truth.
The moment we shed light on nature's
mysteries, the more it will change before
our eyes. The mind is plagued with
being human and can never come to
terms with our humanity. Why seek a
purpose that is half full of meaning?
The human spirit yearns for conscious
freedom, but the heart will never
give up its desires. Hidden truth
has walked out into the light,
and the spirit has become a
blaze of fire.

Let It Go

Can we feel the wind rush through
our hair? The hand's touch has
split our spirit from our body.
Shall we listen to the words that
grow in truth of self-awareness?
Nature's eye is open for the entire
world to see. It will give us the
sole grace to bask in the infinite
colors of light's creative will. Is
there harmony in our being, as
we reflect on the grandness of the
world in our awakened state?

The first of Spring, dewdrops cling
on the surface of our existence and
cover us in a haze of delight. Our
soul is the flower that grows within
us, awakening in the dawn of
light. Let go of human perfection;
become the wind of nature's
calling. Time will grind
our steps as gravity rubs our
soles to the ground. How can
one walk on feet that move
against the will to tomorrow?
Youth has grown old in our
fleeting laughter and bears the
lines of old age. How can we
chase the invisible wind that slips
right through our open hands?

Shall we bow down to the roots
of our existence as our thoughts
drift away from awareness? How
can we grow into eternal light
as we wait for divine wisdom to
set us free? The blackbird has
taken to the sky, spreading his
mischievous song, telling
morning to break free from the
silence of night. How can we
open our eyes to the depth of
limitless blue sky? In the stream
of endless clouds, our fate walks in
all directions, iron-willed with somber
certainty. How do we sandwich our
existence between space of Heaven
and Earth? What will a thousand
daffodils do when the wind wills them
to dance in ecstatic burst of emotions?
Let the butterflies spread their
colors into the freshness of
the summer breeze.

The wind holds strong as each
blade of grass bows in grace, in
humble surrender. Can we look
into the face of reality and let go
of our passions that remain
hidden in our senses? Ours is
the time that stirs the rustling
leaves and brings them into a

symphony of soulful laughter.
We have travelled far on our
blessed journey, and in glory,
nature awaits our return.

Oh, fair wind, the world lives
through you, and you walk into
the valley of dreams unfurled. Will
you kindle the heart of eternity
with your hands before the sparks
of reality burn away our
forgotten world?

A Moment of Remembrance

A moment spreads into the wind and
stirs the imagination that lets fly
too many wings. Calm breaks the
glass of silence, as all eyes look
into the light in search of full
harmony. Night sings our
faithful song in a voice of dreamy
reflection, a vivid scene of forgotten
days; the world is no longer simple.
We linger to hear our heart's
laughter as mournful tears fall
quickly on the blessed face
of reality. We are born into our
human grace as we learn to
grow with eternal time. This is the
time when we are lost in the great mass
of humanity. This is the time when
innocence is seduced into ripened age.

The mind holds too many thoughts,
and the heart no longer listens to
the voice of wisdom. Where are
the waves of our ocean that
emotions bring to shore? What
becomes of blood that is soaked
in human suffering? Like a comedy
that cuts deep into our truth
we hold on to too many follies;
we hold on to too many
dreams. In time when we
run too fast, the pillars of
reality blur their form in
washed-out light. Like sand
pressed into form, we wash
away too much existence.

Like a shadow that won't let light
go, we have forgotten to close
our eyes. The beauty of nature
rubs too hard; the vision of life
seems too distant. Are we of
happy mold? Are we of
sculptured form? How willfully
we surrender to our sensual
needs. How moody the fragrance
of life has become. The spirit of our
will is lost in child's play as we
try to become children once
more. How do we bring back
these joyful moments? How do we
overcome the torment of freedom?

Can we escape through our heart
to touch the sky? In our conscious
ways we look deeply into light, as
colors of the world reflect through
our soul. Into the valley, the strong
wind blows, as fast-flowing rivers
cut through rocky mountains. Can
we see beyond the allure of our
veiled reality? How can beauty
be undying in these unforgiving
hands of time? How will it lead
us into tomorrow's song? How will
we come to know and remember our
forgotten name? Who is it that walks
through our doors? Where are
the lost moments that our
dreams bring to shore?

A Word Too Many

***

If you love the sounds and
colors of all seasons, then
the heart of this world will see
you in light of reason.

***

Your insight seeks refuge from
curiosity, but how curious is
thought when curiosity
becomes so insightful?
A mind that wanders curiously
is not elusive, but mindful.

***

If the senses could see the
world solely, this world
would reflect back to us
with smiling eyes.
In this light the shadow
lives in our body, but
in darkness the soul
never dies.

***

To dream is to feel night's glory,
but to awaken from a dream is glory
everlasting.
A life that lives for a purpose
is enriched in spirit and always
enchanting.

***

Holding that which you can't
relinquish is when losing it binds
you to its eternal longing.
A life that is lived in simplicity
holds truly the secrets
of life's belonging.

***

A shadow loves light as it
gives life its colorful form.
The human spirit can never
be free until the will of the
mind is born.

***

If we choose to run away
from truth, walking
among friends runs the
risk of blasphemy.
Only a hypocrite walks
with pride in a heart
full of agony.

***

Those who feel the torment
of freedom have not been prisoners
in freedom's torment.
Let the spirit break free from
the will of humanity and you will never
look back and lament.

***

If you give me the joy of living, then
I will remove the darkness
from your light.

How can you bargain with reality
when you become the soul
of the night?

***

If we see what God sees,
our religious convictions
will be of no consequence.
In faith, our will is strong as
we walk away from temptation
with full confidence.

***

To feel the height of one's accomplishment
one should walks away from pride
with an even head.
The humble spirit will lose no ground
as one prepares for the
journey ahead.

***

An observation fails to be observed
once the intent to observe
is there.
One won't see what he wants
to see if he gives the world a
blank stare.

***

If truth could reveal its true character, then
this mask of reality would surely be known.
Your deeds will give you character and build
you from flesh and bones.

***

If a heart could desire its hearty desires,
then this hearty soul would
suffer less heartache.
The soul can do no wrong, but

living in our body is our
first mistake.

***

Beauty holds captive that
which seems beautiful.
A lover expresses thoughts
that beauty finds
truthful.

***

The one who seeks can journey too
far, but seeking far-away things
brings us closer to knowledge.
If we seek truth within truth, then
we destroy the realm of fallacy
our heart won't acknowledge.

***

In time of need, let your ego be
absolved; what you may get
back is your needless self.
Those who give to others
gain wealth of pleasure
within themselves.

***

The one who wills his life
will achieve a willful living.
Can one trust a heart
that is all-forgiving?

***

Can we stir the water until life's
sweetness touches our lips?
We often become a drop in our
ocean, a prisoner on our own ship.

***

To know that which knows you best
is to see one's reflection reflect back
with reflecting eyes.
Your home is never yours
when you live in walls of lies.

***

The cruelest of intentions deserves the
friendliest response when good intentions
have evil motives.
Extend your hand to your true enemy with
good faith; the world will notice.

***

In moments of reflection, you
will reflect your light a
thousand times.
Let the world become a
verse of your poetic vision
in rhythm and in rhymes.

***

The pleasure of life seems
pleasing only when one is
pleased with oneself.
What does it cost to smile
at others and at yourself?

***

If you judge others it
will deflect back on you.
True judgment is never yours;
it's the standard of two.

***

If you define your will
the hand will be your master.
Fate lies in one's actions;
pace your life a little faster.

***

True wisdom speaks softly in
quiet overtones.
Your will is like a hammer to
senses made of stones.

***

You will burn the forest if
you are dry in spirit. It is
the spark of inspiration
that will turn you into ashes.
This is the truth the wind
picks up with a whisper as
your soul awakens from
the embers of your eternal
passion.

***

Life spent on an intellectual
journey knows no bounds.
The deeper you go into knowledge
the more ignorant you will sound.

***

The colors of life hold
one open to all eternity.
Oh, nature you have given your
heart to this jaded world with
loving hands of serenity.

***

Spark of Hope

The stars' glitter awakens the
spirit, and shades of moonlight
become our blanket for the
night. In the stillness of a river,
trees whisper into the mystery
of life and awaken the soul's eye.
Shall we let nature immerse in
our senses and walk beside us into
our worldly dreams? On our journey,
we lose our way as we walk
on roads that lead nowhere.

Look into the face of nature, and
beauty will reflect deeply in our
senses. The window to eternity is
half-open, half-closed, but we
will to open it all the way. Will
we welcome the wandering
spirit that comes knocking at our
door? Will we find our form as
candle's light liberates our fate
from our heart of darkness?

The road through life takes many
turns, as we hope to come home
someday. In one moment, we
are called the hopeful, and the
roots of our being grow beyond
that with which we can cope. Will
we become the light within our fire,
the spark of all enduring hope?

Open-Minded

The answers to our will are
written on the pages of destiny.
How will we grow from seeds
of consciousness and awaken as
the hidden soul of reality? Let
the inner light grow into our
being, as we come to realize
our awareness. Can we ever
find true form in our
deep lines of sorrow?

Can we ever forgive the one who
has never been forgiven? In
life, we escape through our
shadow and become a prisoner
in freedom. We are the crest in
our wave, foaming with emotions,
striving for the sandy shore. The mind
awakens the soul and questions
the will of our body to live. Will we
grant the wisdom to our life that
fate has failed to give?

Words

Words will become the soul
of our wisdom and echo into our
world with meaningful existence.
We are born blind into our words;
the way of life will speak its truth.
The shades of darkness hold our
words to light as they fall heavily
onto conscious will. Words have
power to break the walls of nations,
holding prisoner the will of the masses.
Our words are no longer ours, but
have become the words of humanity.

The words of our mind have escaped
our tongue and awaken the moral eye
of human civilization. Aged with
time, our words ripen and echo back
full of revelation and meaning.
Will we recognize such words when
they call out to our forgotten soul?
Humbled by these words is the grace
of creation that frees us from our
ignorant ways. Words will lift the
wings of freedom and rise above
the will of evil. We are bound by
the laws of nature; words will
nurture our true being.

Moral seeds are sown in
our words and grow into the
human spirit. Words less spoken
will retrace our steps in every
moment of life's journey. Under
the veil of hidden reality, words
will whisper to our heart the
love that will never die. Can
we balance our words on the
scale of experience? Our words
have come of age and have
become the tongue of our
intelligence.

Cleansed Soul

Let the soft water touch our
lips and awaken the spirit of
youth. In our quest for meaning,
we feel like a drop within the
ocean as we struggle to overcome
the depth of shallow needs. Human
existence is the holy bread of
life's miracle. Will we breathe
in consciousness and hold it
against our will? With these
eyes we seek our reflection,
a vision of reality that truly
opens our senses.

We walk into spirit enlightened,
as our shadow lingers and holds
firm. How much is our life worth
in silver and gold? The wealth of
humanity will know the truth only
when we strive to overcome poverty.
The vision of life comes into nature's
poetic creation, once self-reflection
comes into awareness. The fate
of reality exists in a mind that
forms the cast for our conscious
soul. We become flesh and bone
in our endless pleasures as the soul
decays and perishes in sorrow.

The will of mind breaks with our
wisdom and seeks emotions that drowns
our heart. There is only wind in our
space, as words fall into the abyss
of hollow sound. Do we feel the grind
of life's friction rub against our
feet? Can we feel the bleeding wounds
of our heart? Can we wash our
face in the water of our own blood?
How can we cleanse our soul in a
world of contradictions? Our lips
have tasted hard water, but
the thirst for bitter existence
has become our only
addiction.

Awaken

Dear love, you have become the
river of emotions that flows
deep in my heart. Long after the
dreamy night you awaken me at
dawn and, like misty dew, I cling to
thy spirit. The pain of longing holds
the spirit fast in joy of sorrow. These
eyes have become silent emotions
in your world, deep-rooted in heart
of separation. Will your face ever touch
the depth of these deep brown eyes?
The wind echoes your name, as
nature fragments in joy and becomes
the sediments of your consciousness.

Your spirit is the only consolation
in this uncaring world. Will you give
me the love that will grow into my
awakened state? On this star-filled
night, the moon burns your image
onto the edges of silver-gray clouds.
Under the stillness of eternity
you make me wait, as you are
nowhere to be found. These eyes
are full of deception as your ghostly
steps are heard on soft blessed ground.
True love thirsts for the ocean and
in your love I will drown
a thousand times.

The spirit of love is born in
one moment of existence as I
fade into the edges of your form.
These eyes trace the horizon as waves
wash me ashore to prostrate at your feet.
Seagulls take flight and sail into the wind.
Clouds walk away from the conscious
eyes as they fade away into the distance.
The calm of the night has been broken
by emotions that fall heavily on my
delicate spirit. The hands of creation
liberate your beauty from the light,
as I cling to the shadow of your form.
The embers of my heart smolder
with every breath you take. I
will give up dreams of eternity
to live in the warmth
of your soul.

Will you look my way as I fade into
the valley of dreams? If life could
give me one moment, a thousand
moments will call your name.
These faithful eyes have opened their
doors to let you in for all time. Will
you embrace this love in a reality
that makes you my only truth?
Only true love is undying,
a scent of everlasting youth.

Metamorphosis

In the vastness of eternity, life gives
joy to each and every moment.
We have been etched into the mold
of time; the metamorphosis of our
spirit turns to flesh. Colors that bathe
our youthful emotions flow deeply
into the heart of a lover's dream. The
hot summer breeze flirts with our
senses to move the heart closer to
the truth of conscious living. Will
we see the child come into being,
skipping stones with small hands
in dazzling motion? Splish-splash, the
flat stone surfs the water, as sound
breaks the stillness of the quietly
moving water and bedazzles its
clear glass surface. Childlike
laughter on the edge of a
winding road weathered in
life has come of age.

In our inner eye, laughter is
serene, but our voice is heavy,
full of earthly wisdom. How will
we face a humanity that no
longer exists? Let emotional joy
become mist in our eyes as we
try to walk through the web of
existence. The wings of our mind
are free-flowing; there is no burden

to hold us under. Into the heart of
nature a butterfly is born, to deepen
the colors of creation. Specks of life
settle like dust, reflecting the silver
light of a thousand dreams.

Give back our youth that was lost too
quickly, as the soul can no longer
bargain with time. The mystical
voice calls us to open the doors and
let the spirit journey home. In the
stillness of eternity, words of our
life will reveal our story. The end
is our beginning, and this beginning
has no end. Let the body become the
bridge to the soul as we walk toward
the fullness of our happiness. In
our journey, our eyes have grown
roots into wisdom. The stone
has come to reflect our water,
and the child holds us in joyful
reflection. We grow out of our
metamorphosis, and what
we are today we will no
longer be tomorrow.

Truth

Truth speaks to one who
listens with an open mind.
True wisdom is the seed
of the soul that grows toward
eternal truth. Hold your light in
the mirror of consciousness,
and truth will escape through the
darkness of human nature. Will
you let the eyes become your
virtuous soul to see far beyond
the unseen truth? Those who
seek the truth willingly will
come to know it. In spirit, life
will lift the burden of reality, as
one walks with righteous steps
toward the beauty of nature. The
humble act of reason will settle
truth deep in your heart. What
the eternal truth of tomorrow can
never be the truth for this moment.

There is no truth in humanity until
the oppressed soul is liberated from
universal suffering. The oneness of
truth is the collective consciousness
of human spirit. Truth will come
full circle when all share the fruit
that it bears. In your water, you
will come to reflect reality as your
face mirrors the heart and faith

of truth. How will you open
your mind to the greater truth?
A soul that builds walls of
hate has no home for truth.
Fragments of true existence shape
your morality as true virtue settles
in eternal youth. Truth shall be
the way to all things, and
all things will move toward
universal truth.

Soaring Spirit

We are born into our world,
but the civility of human
nature is not our destined
path. The caste of nobility
is the old custom for the rich.
We have become the mud in
our water, unworthy of the
mold that gives us form. In the
majesty of our open sky, the soul
becomes transparent, but in
body it has become opaque. Let
our spirit become the house of
nature. Our eyes of perception have
no doors; light walks in unhindered.
The colors of life bathe our senses,
as reality awakens our mind.
We are guests in this cold, hard
world, there are no realms whose
walls will protect us. We lift our
spirit into the vastness of the sapphire
sky and take a moment to breathe.

Who can love reason that holds no
truth? In our great love we become
the arms of freedom. Those
who love will glow in light of
a beautiful dream. Love that parts
too quickly leaves us empty for all
eternity. In this endless longing, the
only true treasure we shall find is

one that binds us to love. Let the
glow of moonlight pave the road
to heaven as night sleeps under the
comfort of untold emotions. Will we
walk into our darkness and fade into
light? We become thus a fragment
of broken consciousness, as words
of humanity penetrate our soul.

How will we collect fragments of
reality to make peace with our
eternal whole? The spirit lives
through our senses until the
senses close all doors to certainty.
Will we falter our spirit against
the doors of time? Heaviness of
footsteps will cut into the soles of
our feet. How far will we journey to
find true love? Emotions will flicker
in our dreamy world as we humble our
eyes to the falling sunset. It is our heart
of stone that we must break, so humanity
can pick up the pieces. We are born
to love, and in love we will never
grow old. Will we ever come to
rest on the surface of reality? Our
fate has willed us to come into
our heart of immortality.

Born Anew

In serenity flows the river
of our substance. We have become
the cradle of our emotions, touched by
the gentle breeze of born-again pleasures.
In passage of time we are held in our
childhood dreams, as we are molded
by the delicate hands of creation.
Our will is revealed and created by
motion of purpose. Dust of destiny we
become; sediments of truth keep
stirring our watery existence. Look into
our venerated eyes, the mind will
not question the ways of our world.
Can we hear the sound of cynical
laughter that gave birth to our name?

Has wisdom not moved the tongue,
to speak silent words that hold no
meaning? The beauty of nature,
virgin and serene, give form to our
sterile world. The soul drowns in
darkness and becomes a prisoner
in the mesh of conscious reality.
Into tomorrow fate will walk,
but destiny will no longer hold
our hands. In faith God is born,
but lost in faith, God becomes
man. On passing roads, life
is restless, as truth fades into the
background of fast-moving time.

Those who strive for eternal
happiness will not find the joy
they seek. We drift into the wind
like fallen leaves, torn by hands
of nature. The world is rustic, empty,
and barren of all that life hopes to give.
Should we jump into the river that drifts
far and deep in our blood? The conscious
soul is conscious of the drop that
falls on the surface of our ocean.
Oh, serenity, why do we cover
our eyes with your hands of
calmness? The body was
born in spirit of purity,
but our ways of living
have become godless.

Tricked

In true wisdom, the fool has become
too wise in human folly. When irony
slips under laughter, truth will come
to light, naked and bare. Why do
fools strive for eternity? Blind
desire have blinded our nature, as
we empty the half-filled bowl of
our existence. In wealth we
loses ourselves and the soul
will be lost forever. We can
become wise if we breathe
in deeply the substance of
our true nature. Only a
fool breathes in water and
drowns in his conscious world.
Those who thirst for air will
hunger for nothing more. Why
seek pleasures that will lead
to no fulfillment? Human
desires have no end, and will
become ruins in burning passion.

Blind to the ways of living, the
human spirit still chases reality
that no longer exists. All wealth
decays and fragments with time.
A heart that is all-giving will
grow rich in poverty. Only a
fool digs deeply into himself
until he digs his own grave.

The wise walk the straight path to
ease their burden, but a fool
will walk with heavy steps
and wander in all directions.
Who among us will see the
heart inside the jewel? Is
it the one who acts the
fool or the one who
breaks all the rules?

Dust in Flame

Those who sow seeds of evil shall
reap no fruit. Like a desert of wasted
sorrow, the seeds will grow no
roots. In the great well of the soul,
the heart, mirrors human nature.
Bitterness of unfulfilled existence
can ripen our aged wisdom.

Under the will of nature, time
will turn and twist our fate
like a fallen leaf. The will
of the spirit tumbles, and light
will breaks through our lines
of insanity. Hands of wisdom
will cut deeply into our face
and mirror our age.
The child will seek comfort
in a mother's embrace. Will
we burn through darkness
to become the ashes of
dust in flame?

Past to Present

The past will etch our steps
into tomorrow. We have walked
through each moment; the road
toward wisdom holds time still.
The stillness of life gives voice to our
words in youthful laughter. Days fold
into nights as dreams transform
our world into a new reality.

Into the deep desolate sky life
takes flight and wings of freedom
lift our spirit into the wind.
Our eyes walk towards light, and in
our perception, the mind is born
anew. In streams of consciousness, the
stillness of dreams falls like sediments
on the surface of reality. How can
senses search through the past to
give form to human grace? In our
journey, light will take us home, but
the spirit will find no refuge. The
mind washes away the footprints
of time and the human soul
is lost to all humanity.

We cannot bargain with time
until we accept our humble beginning;
youth is fast and fleeting, but our
old age is stubborn and long.
The soul has come home to rest,

but the body is nowhere to be found.
Can we lift the anchor that holds
us to our past? In our vision
of tomorrow, our eyes seek the
light of today. In the conscious
mirror of self-reflection, we become
trapped in our web of reality that
we have created. A life that strives
for simplicity will seek only the humble
truth. We search for time wasted,
but find us lost in reality.

We hold in our hands the strings of life;
it swings the pendulum from past to
present. Rest in this "now" moment
to enjoy the breeze that makes
the journey warm and pleasant.

Humanity

In the spirit of living, the heart
will bow to our will and remain
open to the fullness of life.
Truth lives in the darkness of
our eyes, but still sheds light
for the whole world to see.
In silent whisper, the mind
reflects on the words of
humanity. In wisdom,
words are never spoken.

Can we breathe in the vastness
of space and hold our breath
in wonder? Can we give truth
the doors to our imagination?
Life has opened the gates to
our senses, and there remains
no will to shatter the moment.
Seduced by tranquility, the
wind calls our name, and
the body falls in line with
our soul. In the depth
of emotions, the eyes will
bow to the shallowness
of our self-reflection. On
firm surface we walk swiftly,
and the open sky swallows us
whole. The night robs us of
all glory as we fall into the
abyss of dreams. Our pride

cuts through humble existence
and tears us into many pieces.
In our will to be human, we
become powerless under the force
of human nature. The soul is
lost in time as humanity
seeks its vanished eternity.
Who is the man inside the
man? What is it to be
human? Let the spirit
first become humane;
then humanity will
never live
in vain.

Seeds of Reality

In the tyranny of reason, the
mind becomes trapped in the will to
be free. The mosaic of reality is in
every part of the whole, and the
whole must see its every part.
Let truth open the doors to let
freedom come into our soul.

Life is a glass reality in our
consciousness, but the form
holds too much light to
liberate the spirit. How will
the mirror of self-reflection
see into our dense nature?
Seeds of reality grow roots
in humanity, as we rise
to the surface fully formed.
How will we come to realize
our non-existence? Nature
transforms what nature
comes to know, and fosters
the beauty it comes to show.
The will to be human is
the hand that holds our
lives close to our faith. Life
is one moment of living and
no other moment will come
our way. Will we smell the
fragrance of life before
the wind takes it away?

What becomes of conscious
reality once it is washed in
nature's water? How will
the soul bargain with the
body's pleasures? How deeply
will we go into ourselves before
we lose touch with reality?
What will life be when the two
ends of existence come full
circle? The mind falls deep into
thought, and the self rises to the
surface fully realized. Our spirit
becomes too vast and restless for our
dreams. Once the heart grows cold
there is no room for peace and justice.
We must destroy the old to give birth
to a new beginning. Is the will to destroy
innate in our human nature? The light of
reality opens the eye of humanity,
and the senses hold no lies. What
will we see when we truly
open our eyes?

Reflection

We seek understanding and
there is no veil of secrecy beyond
our name. Nature became our
true witness, and there is so much
our hearts want to share. How
deep will life run in our blood? How
much life's fragrance dissolves
into the wind when we run fast
toward the infinite soul? The
craving for life will burn the light
of darkness that lies beyond
our soul. Behind our eyes we
will hold our true face.
Awareness will give one life
once we begin to live. Let the
river be our truth and in time
it will walk into our ocean
fully realized. In mountains
of dreams, we are humbled
to the ground as we grow
into the landscape like
trees in the forest.

We will never be understood
until we break away from
our reflection and run
toward the light. There is
no wisdom in a life that
holds no purpose and gives
no hope to the human

spirit. In true love, we are born, and, through love, we become whole. Will we listen to our heart and do its bidding? Our fate will humble in wisdom and sincerity as we bow in prayers to every moment the Lord grants and gives. Our simple thoughts put our minds at ease; no weight can burden them. If reality ties us in a knot, ours will be a tangled path. A thirst for life will free our soul; then we are truly born. As the mind opens the doors, what wishes to be known shall be shown.

Light Touch

When will we let light escape
through our darkness? True
wisdom has no feet, but it can walk
into our heart with silent steps.
We shall unite with what we see,
when light touches the surface
of our conscious soul. When will
we shed our faith, and give our life
a new reality? There is no real life
when we live beneath the shadow
of dreams. The spirit is soaked
in humanity, there is too much
burden to overcome human
gravity. The night has become
the canvas for our dreams, as
consciousness sleeps and time
holds still. What is the force
that gives light the impulse to
move? What will we find when
light awakens our inner eye?

Let there be light in darkness.
Let embers of emotion smolder
and burn on the road we long to
travel. Youthful laughter echoes
in the wind and returns with
new wisdom. The light of the
spirit comes into our eyes with
moments of inner-certainty.
Will we walk into ourselves,
and move into the dawn of
a new day? We are born into
existence for but a moment
to touch awareness before
we fade away.

By SHAKOOR

Arise

In a moment of sadness,
the mist of hope that blankets
the withered soul arises.
Was it not in heart's sorrow
that we found our true
spirit? It is the ocean that
runs in our tears as we
drown in our emotions with
each breath we take. How
will our senses take in
the fragrance of true love?

Who is capable of love in a
world that holds too many
promises? The joy in sorrow
gives the soul more room
for happiness. Slow and heavy
are footsteps that one takes,
as we carry the weight of
purpose deep into our soul.
Our life is a spark of creation
that ignites the imagination
in our awareness of perception.
The spirit is reborn a thousand
times when soaked in the water of
existence. Let the mind open the
conscious eye to help us find our way.

Where human sorrows end,
there begins the birth of true
happiness. Sorrow binds
emotions to the strong will
of mind. A mystical voice
echoes the call. The root
of happiness springs from
the seeds of sorrow. Will
you arise beyond stagnation
and look for the light
in hope for tomorrow?

Eternal Love

Life gives substance to the
body, but it is through love
that the soul is born. Love
is found in one moment
of time but is a lifetime
in the making. We may
love only once but be
in love forever. The
spirit glows in the light
of love and becomes the
hope of the world.
Eternal light will lead
us on the path to everlasting
love. Love is measured in all
things, and all things are
measured through love.

A thousand stars sparkle in
glory to burn away the darkness
of the mystical night. How far
must we journey to trace
the path to love? Will our eyes
bow, as we pray to the heavens
above? Our love lives in
the heart of a thousand
lovers, all consumed
in the oneness of
eternal love.

Half-Empty

We are born into the
empty bowl of existence.
The cup of life is full,
but we thirst for curiosity
of all-knowing. We grow
deep in awareness and the
soul awakens us. The light
of reality has come home
to our senses to voice the
truth of wisdom. The world
is full of color and dreams
as we look into ourselves
in wonder. Will we savor
the sweet aftertaste
on our lips?

The bowl is half-empty
in a soul but half
full in a spirit that seeks
life's fulfillment. In
one spur moment of happiness,
our life will emit light
a thousand times strong.
The human spirit is
realized in self-love, and
will grow in the mind
of humanity. Though we
might feel insignificant,
infinite reality gives
us relevance.

A wise spirit can travel
deeply into meaning,
but often returns to the
surface light and simple.
In God's truth, you are a
mind of divine wisdom.
We will rise again in a
forest that humanity
has burned; the soul
of creation is life's
moment of infinity
lost and infinity
regained.

Oh, Daughter

In the purity of human
spirit, you shed your
light and become the
vision that rests on the
surface of my soul. The
colors of life blend into
my days as you become
a mother's joy spreading
out into the world.

The fullness of eternity
beats in your heart as
memories race back to
my youthful days. Like
ivory snow your childish
virtue tickles my flesh into
a warm shiver. Filled
with love from heaven,
you embrace my spirit
with total tranquility.

You are the mirror of
my existence. Veiled in
nature's beauty are colors
of reality, and God's miracle
of creation. The glorious sun
breaks through the summer
breeze and you become the
joyful daffodil dancing in
my world. You have given

honey sweetness to maternal love. I will walk in your footsteps on your road to womanhood. Under the vast blue open sky, your serene face lifts the spirit of my world. In motherly love you have become wings of happiness, my precious dove. Oh, daughter! You have unlocked the doors to heaven in your endless love.

Beauty of Nature

A mist of white covers the
soft landscape of the evergreen.
The cold blue silky sky shivers
under the vastness of reality.
Like a caravan marching
endlessly, distant clouds
walk through the house
of nature. On the canvas
of a slow-moving river,
the beauty of color reflects
the soul of creation. Distilled
in motion of time, trees
remain frozen in their
tracks, weighing the burden
of their stillness. Soft virgin
snow cries over lonely mountains,
letting its tears give birth to
icy rivers. Will you look deep
into the miracle of life, as
nature calls to humanity
to open their eyes to the
world and see its glory?
Heaven's voice calls
from a distance to echo
the sounds and sweetness
of this mystical world. The
wind, restless with emotions,
stirs leaves into a laughter-filled
dream. A thousand echoes
break through the surface
of reality and run through
the caves of your soul. Will
nature settle into the sediments
of consciousness the beauty of life
that makes us whole?

Mystery of Moonlight

The moon was breaking through the endless
streams of dark clouds,
and the wind was watching all this and
standing proud.
Trees with outreaching branches
began to bathe in the ivory glow;
shadows took form and shades of strange
colors began to show.
Silent was the world when all this
was taking place,
as the mystery of moonlight held the earth
in a nightly embrace.

Face of Beauty

Oh, beauty, your face has many
forms that glimpse in and out
of life's inner-world. Like mystery
that holds charm, you have
become the heart of a lover's
dream. Like the scent of a
flower you take hold of
the wind but still remain a
thorn to the touch. Will you
let your fragrance spill
into the breeze and stir
the emotions as such?

Your soft features are carved
out of darkness through the eye of a
candle's light. The feeble heart
will not confess its forbidden love and
keeps drinking the poison in endless thirsts.
Beauty will hold you deep as the warm
moonlit night brings you into the
moment lined with age. In time,
you will grow into beauty and
break free from your
hidden cage.

Humility

A man is a mountain of dreams who lingers
upon the shadow of his own reflection.
A destructive soul of his own making, he
creates monuments to his own perfection.
Human desires are the enemy of human
wisdom trapped in their inner wars.
Fate of humanity is the prisoner of time,
a dwindling light among the stars.
A speck of dust is age of being, as you
bow to pride with a humble nod.
Laws of nature gave you form,
as your soul comes back to God.

Empathy

I held her hand in sincerity as she
held mine with apprehension.
I looked into her eyes as she looked
into mine. The silent gesture of defeat
betrayed my face. My voice quivered,
as words broke forth. With eyes
lowered I told of her cancer; it was
malignant. A tear fell from her eye
and she could not hold it from falling.
I touched her soul and felt her heart
break through my own doing.

Her suffering was lined with pain and
she knew her suffering well. I felt
her sorrow run through my soul
like a tortured river running toward
deep vast ocean. I gave her my
full kindness as she turned away and
looked into the light. She searched
for hope in her faith and I searched for
my faith lost with time. Her heavy
heart bled with emotions as her
broken dreams drifted like withered
leaves scattered by the wind. She
asked if there was any chance of cure.
I could not bring myself to playing
God. She accepted her fate with her
half smiling face, but I could not come
to terms with my fate. Her spirit broke
through this glass certainty and gave

strength to her great moment of
weakness.

The reality was broken into many
pieces, but she gathered her courage
to take them home. The cancer
had overtaken her body, but her spirit
remained strong. She looked over my
face in silence, took my hand and wished me
well. Her quiet steps diminished as they
traced life's fragile existence. The day
settled in silent time and sentiments came
to surface, no longer benign. She lingered
deep in my thoughts long after the
dim glow of sunshine.

Adore

The world will adore our
spirit that opens our heart
to the joy of living. Each
instant reflects steps
into life's journey that
are all-giving. Our soul
spreads our fragrance
to the wind and awakens
us into night's glory. The
world becomes a symphony of
music as we listen for the
sounds of nature's story.

The colors of life give form to
our emotions mixed in love.
Our dreams drift into the
night to become the wings
to heaven above. Our eyes
hold light in elusive shades
of reality and give comfort
to our wandering soul. The
heart thirsts for fulfillment
and reflects emotions
in our half-filled bowl.

Braided in dark twilight of
night, fate has tied us in a
knot. The heart holds no
secrets, and unravels the
mystical plot. In our mind

rest the creative words
of destiny. The purity of true
love washes the world with
harmony. Deep emotions
that burn on our lips give
life all their meaning. With
every breath, we breathe in
existence and give our wisdom
a new beginning. In our cold,
hard world, the only solace
for heart is to rest our face
in a lover's arms. Hands of
eternity will hold us close
and buffer us from life's
bitter charm. The footsteps of
longing come knocking at our
door. In endless search, the
heart will seek none but the
one we truly adore.

Story

Spoken words linger on
hushed lips longing to break our
silence. The heart is cold, but
the spirit is warm. In our empty
eyes, the joy of living has found
its home. The wind brings back
the secrets of life and holds
memories under our moments of
reflection. Can love ever break
the heart of nature and remain
unbroken? Will humanity ever
find wisdom in light that burns
without truth? Listen to the
sound of your own laughter; it
will bring your eyes to tears.

In vastness of our imagination
we become aware of our peaceful
face. Deep on the surface of
our consciousness, the inner eye
has no desires, seeks no treasures.
Where will time take us when the
soul seeks too much space? Will we
let the shadow chisel into our form
and bring out the stubborn will?
How can we live in freedom when we
forget to hold our breath underwater?

Give up your existence and become
the guest of this world. We are born

in our moment of eternity to seek
our infinite ways. Life has become
a vision of reality to our woken
eye. How can we face our illusions
when reality of mind is no longer
real? Sounds of silence echo back
from the walls of consciousness.
Have we come to terms with
our contradictions that trap
us in our self-importance?
Can we pen through our
empty pages to write our
story? Give your words
wings to touch the sky
in vision and in glory.

Final Thought

The momentum of life will move
us forward as we try never to
look back. We have become
like the wind, touching our
thoughts silently, empty-handed,
and with no will for direction.
The steps of reality have moved
to the side as we wander and seek
the road toward our destiny.

The ifs and buts of doubt have
escaped our mind's prison. The
doors to certainty have opened
our will. We have no desire to
walk on our shadow, but to
run and fade into the humble
light of imperfection. Will
we do the undoable and bear
the hardship of life and overcome
pride? Shed your existence into
consciousness, and become the
soul of the human spirit. Can we
open our eyes and look deep into
blindness? Words less spoken will
overflow with emotion, as our
heart seeks meaning in love.
We are a mosaic in fragmented
time as we try to piece together
our broken dreams. To
become relevant in our

universe we must give
and not receive.

There will be time to
labor, and time to fall
in love with life. The
spirit will glow with joy
and laughter once light
touches our center.
Like broken leaves that
fall onto the surface of
reality, time will collect
the grains of sand day
and night. So, smile at
the hours of life, for this
time is ours to keep.

Life becomes a river of
wasting when we pursue
dreams that are too
big or too small. All
reality becomes blurred
when we run too fast,
seeking to fulfill our
countless needs. Slow
your steps; don't run
into life too fast.

Those who seek perfection
will cease to exist in their
perfect world. The human

spirit that finds wisdom
in simplicity will gain
its humble existence. Those
who give themselves to
others will gain something
more in return. The full
meaning of success and
failure become alike when
we accept all things that
come our way. We are
guests in our world,
born into our beginning
to live toward our end;
none are here to stay.
Time is eternal and we
are but a moment of
passing, striving for
fulfillment and purpose
with every passing day.

Made in the USA
Monee, IL
01 October 2020

43427405R00145